RESEARCH BIBLIOGRAPHIES & CHECKLISTS

19

The Poetry of Alfonso X, el Sabio

RESEARCH BIBLIOGRAPHIES & CHECKLISTS

R&B

General editors

A. D. Deyermond, J. R. Little and J. E. Varey

THE POETRY OF
ALFONSO X, EL SABIO

a critical bibliography

by

JOSEPH SNOW

Grant & Cutler Ltd
1977

❂ Grant & Cutler Ltd
1977

ISBN 0 7293 0042 0

I.S.B.N. 84-399-8417-0

DEPÓSITO LEGAL: V. 1.688 - 1978

Printed in Spain by Artes Gráficas Soler, S.A., Valencia

for

GRANT & CUTLER LTD
11, BUCKINGHAM STREET, LONDON, W.C.2.

CONTENTS

for

Lloyd A. Kasten

el sabio

INTRODUCTION

The position of great importance that Alfonso X (1221-84) of Castile and León occupies in the history of the development of the Castilian language is well known and has been widely commented, especially as regards the writing of prose: its grammar, its rhythms, and even its orthography owe much to the precepts formulated by Alfonso X and practised in the royal scriptorium. Much more surprising are claims, such as the one by Eugenio Asensio (see *infra*, item 260), that make Alfonso the founder of the Castilian poetic tradition. For with the exception of one fragmentary poem in his native Castilian, the remainder of the poetry — some 465 or so compositions — are in Galician-Portuguese, the normal idiom for writing lyric and satirical poems in much of the Iberian Peninsula in the thirteenth century. As if in support of Asensio, both Le Gentil (no. 221) and Clarke (no. 251) tell us that all the verse forms used in fifteenth-century *cancioneros* are present in Alfonso's *Cantigas de Santa Maria* (*CSM*).

Alfonso's poetry ought to be considered the common property of the literatures of both Spain and Portugal. This becomes particularly clear if one considers the evolution of poetry and poetic forms in the two centuries 1250-1450. The entire picture is far too complex to deal with here; however, if we remember that the bulk of Alfonso's poetry was composed in the first three decades of this period we can understand how important a bridge it is between the last flowering of the Provençal manner and the later revival of its essential elements in the Peninsular *cancioneros*. Alfonso is not the only link in the chain, but he certainly must be considered, in the light of the poetic activity at his own court and of the inspiration provided for the court of his grandson, Dinis of Portugal, the essential link. No poet of his time or after contributed so many poems nor attained such prestige as a poet and sponsor of poets, not even Dinis who is often called the last of the important Galician-Portuguese poets. Alfonso, on the other hand, wrote at the very summit of the creative powers of that poetic idiom. Not long after Alfonso, and at about the same time as Dinis, we have the evidence of the *Libro de buen amor* that Castilian had indeed acquired its own lyric voice. Yet poets continued to write in Galician-Portuguese as well as in Castilian until gradually, in the late fourteenth century, the Castilian poetic idiom could be considered triumphant over the then moribund Galician (Portuguese having become an independent and vital linguistic entity of its own). But in effect, the gap between the two traditions in the Peninsula probably was never so small as in the latter part of the thirteenth century. Alfonso's *CSM*, though composed in Galician-Portuguese, is innovative in one important way: there was no prior tradition of religious song on which to model *cantigas*. Alfonso created those for himself, perhaps not *ex nihilo*, but certainly with a great deal of concern for what he was about. He had, after all, also participated in the satirical, ribald and even scabrous games of more conventional types of poetry practised by Peninsular poets, and contributed some noteworthy amatory verse as well. This was not all palace poetry either. In fact, much of what Alfonso writes in both the religious and secular poems identifies with the musical and metrical schemes of the poetry most likely to appeal to the populace at large, so that it may be said that he is preparing the way for later generations of poets to finish what he had begun: the creation of a Castilian poetic tradition.

If Alfonso's role in this transition was so vital, then a full review of studies of his poetic production is needed. At this point, enough comment and scholarly investigation has been produced at all levels of merit to justify a full-length bibliography. In 1933, José Sánchez Pérez, one of the earliest of Alfonsine bibliographers, stated: "Cuando llegue la ocasión de realizar el estudio particular de cada una de las facetas de la cultura [de Alfonso], será necesario ampliar esta bibliografía con muchas obras relacionadas con el estudio crítico ... " (no. 152, p. 188). For the poetry of Alfonso X, this bibliography is an attempt to do what Sánchez Pérez knew would have to be done some day.

I have presented, in one chronological listing, all the materials that I could locate. Many of these items are rare; several do not appear in any other bibliography of Alfonsine criticism. Others are quite well known; a few are universally recognized as essential. I have deliberately retained a small number of quite useless items because they appear in other bibliographies without caveats and they deserve to be exposed at last. I can think of many ways in which this bibliography could have been expanded, e.g., by the inclusion of works on poets and poetic styles which adorned Alfonso's court, but I have deliberately not done so. The primary need is to treat the studies on Alfonso as poet and there is abundant material on that alone for the present. The other poets and the prevailing poetic styles are, in point of fact, mentioned often in the entries included in this bibliography and the user will be led to them naturally, finding enough additional bibliography in their notes, etc., to enable him to conduct his own lateral searching. I was tempted to include models for new Alfonsine studies such as the excellent volume by Rosemary Woolf, *The English Religious Lyric in the Middle Ages* (Oxford: Clarendon, 1968), but found they were too many. I have also put aside some reference works which do not study Alfonsine poetry but which could be used with profit for some aspects of its study. Most of these are already familiar to the scholar, works such as Stith Thompson's *Motif-Index of Folk Literature*, revised and enlarged in 6 vols (Bloomington: Univ. of Indiana Press, 1955-8), which incorporates many items from Spanish literature not in the first edition, and the immensely useful series of articles by Adolfo Mussafia published under the general title of "Studien zu den mittelalterlichen Marien-legenden" (Sitzungsberichte der Kaiserlichen Akademie der Wissenschaften, Philosophisch-Historische Classe, Vienna, CXIII (1886), 917-94; CXV (1888), 5-92; CXIX (1899), Abh. 9, 66 pp.; CXXIII (1891), Abh. 8, 85 pp; CXXXIX (1898), Abh. 8, 74 pp.).

The format of the single chronological listing makes possible an easily-accessible outline of the history of the critical appraisal of Alfonso's poetry. In addition to the *CSM* and the *cantigas profanas* Alfonso has also been credited with, at one time or another, the writing of a long poem ("Declaratio") in Provençal which was probably penned by Guiraut Riquier, the spurious *Libro de las querellas*, the *Libro de Alexandre*, the *Libro del tesoro*, and the ballad, "Yo salí de mi tierra". I have included all valuable references to these works (they are not numerically overwhelming) and to the legends surrounding Alfonso: they fit very nicely indeed into the historical approach adopted for the study of Alfonso's poetry.

Such an arrangement has encouraged me to make frequent cross references to other articles on the same topic and I refer to these by the year under which they are listed. As a further supplement to this internal cross-referencing, I have provided, at the end of the bibliography, a Subject Index of the annotations. In order to make this listing useful to scholars who are accustomed to an alphabetical arrangement, I have also supplied an Index of Scholars. The entries for a single year are, of course, arranged alphabetically.

Entries are normally listed under the date when they were first available to scholarship, usually, but not always, their date of publication. Studies which appear in several volumes are most often classed under the year of publication of the first volume: this is particularly true if the volumes represent continuing commentary, e.g. Michaëlis de Vasconcellos (1896), Machado and Le Gentil (both 1949), and Mettmann (1959). Exceptions are volumes which are a part of a series but contain distinct materials or approaches, e.g. Ribera (1922) and the 3 vols of Anglés's study of the music of the *CSM* (1943, 1958 and 1964).

In the case of the annotations I have prepared, it must be admitted that they do serve a wide range of purposes, almost always dictated by the nature of the material and the potential scholarly interest in it. One can expect a summary of content and, variously, critical assessments, notes of errors, a listing of poems treated in the entry, references to other works, authors or themes that are germane to the main point of the item being reviewed, and a mini-index of locations of poetic material when no index is provided by the author or editor.

For the *CSM*, unless otherwise stated, all numbers are those of Mettmann's ed. (1959-64). No easy solution was possible for the *cantigas profanas* since so many different systems were used, and not to have preserved, in the annotations, the numbers used in the item concerned would have led to great confusion. I have prepared Appendix A as an aid to unravelling these numbers and its consultation ought to save much time. The scholar interested in where a certain *cantiga* might have previously been commented upon should consult Appendix B.

I have standardized certain features throughout. The place of publication is in English. An author whose name is given in different forms is listed in the manner attached to his more important contributions; thus, Higinio Anglés and not Higini Anglès, José Filgueira Valverde and not Xosé Filgueira Valverde. When no publisher could be determined from an investigation of all the imprint information, I have included the printer as a substitute. I have respected the spelling conventions of the titles throughout.

Finally, there has been a large amount of support given to me during the two years or so while this bibliography was in the making.

Diana Rineer was a student assistant in the early stages and helped prepare *fichas* and check on the accuracy of some of the items located at the Univ. of Georgia Libraries. The staff of the latter institution, especially M. Ellis, B. Herbert, S. Morris, and M. Yeager of the Dept of Inter-Library Loans, worked long and hard to help me locate many unusual items. Dr John Dowling, Head of the Romance Languages Dept at the Univ. of Georgia, believed in this project and committed funds towards the costs of xeroxing and the purchase of materials obtained through the Inter-Library Loan. My colleagues, Profs J. Torres Fontes, N.B. Smith and P.T. Johnson obtained materials for me that would otherwise have been absent from this bibliography; R. McCormick and Profs Erna Berndt Kelley and Wolfgang Binder generously helped with some difficult German items. Last, and not least, Prof. A.D. Deyermond, editor of this series, encouraged and nourished this project, was patient and tolerant of delays, and shared home and office so that it might be finished. To all of these people I wish to record my debt and to express my sincere, deep thanks for their several positive contributions. Of course, I alone must bear any responsibility for that which is missing or in error.

J.T. Snow
University of Georgia

October, 1976

ABBREVIATIONS

In addition to the abbreviations listed here, I have often found it convenient to abbreviate the author's name, using the initial of the surname(s), e.g. Jones becomes J., and Menéndez Pidal becomes M.P.

AION-SR	*Annali dell'Istituto Orientale di Napoli - Sezione Romanza*
AUCh	*Anales de la Universidad de Chile*
BH	*Bulletin Hispanique*
BN	Biblioteca Nacional - Madrid
BRAE	*Boletín de la Real Academia Española*
BRAH	*Boletín de la Real Academia de la Historia*
CA	*Cancioneiro da Ajuda*
CB	*Cancioneiro Colocci-Brancuti*
CBN	*Cancioneiro da Biblioteca Nacional* (Lisbon)
ch.	chapter
CSIC	Consejo Superior de Investigaciones Científicas
CSM	*Cantigas de Santa Maria*
CV	*Cancioneiro da Vaticana*
d.	died
DAI	*Dissertation Abstracts International* (previous to July, 1969, called *Dissertation Abstracts*)
doc(s).	document(s)
FM	*Festas de Santa Maria*
HR	*Hispanic Review*
Impta	Imprenta
KRQ	*Kentucky Romance Quarterly*
MLN	*Modern Language Notes*
MLR	*Modern Language Review*
MRAE	*Memorias de la Real Academia Española*

MS, MSS	manuscript(s)
NRFH	*Nueva Revista de Filología Hispánica*
prol.	prologue
RABM	*Revista de Archivos, Bibliotecas y Museos*
RAE	Real Academia Española
RAH	Real Academia de la Historia
RDTP	*Revista de Dialectología y Tradiciones Populares*
RF	*Romanische Forschungen*
RFE	*Revista de Filología Española*
RoN	*Romance Notes*
Tip.	Tipografía
ZRP	*Zeitschrift für Romanische Philologie*

THE POETRY OF ALFONSO X, EL SABIO

1278

1 Gil de Zamora, Fr. Juan (writing *ca* 1278), cited in Fidel Fita, "Biografías de San Fernando y de Alfonso el Sabio por Gil de Zamora", *BRAH,* V (1884), 308-28.
Gil de Zamora must be counted as Alfonso's first professional critic: he was a poet and a theoretician of music at Alfonso's court. From the art. above, p. 321: "adeo quoque animum suum transtulit ad investigandas et perscrutandas mundanas scientias et divinas, quod omnes fere scripturas triviales et quadriviales, canonicas et civiles, scripturas quoque theologicas seu divinas transferri fecit in linguam maternam; ita et omnes possent evidentissime intueri et intelligere quoquomodo illa, que sub lingue latine phaleris et figura tecta et secreta, etiam ipsis sapientibus, videbantur. *More quoque Davitico etiam, ad preconium Virginis gloriose multas et perpulchras composuit cantinelas, sonis convenientibus et proportionibus musicis modulatas*". Perhaps the only independent contemporary evidence of direct intervention in texts and music by Alfonso.

1588

2 Argote de Molina, Gonzalo, *Noblezas del Andaluzia* (Madrid, 1588), libro II, ch. XVI, fols 151v-154r.
An account of the transfer of the *CSM* to the Escurial library at the order of Felipe II. To shed light on another event of his own time, Argote transcribes *cantiga* 185 which contains an analogous situation. Certainly one of the earliest eye-witness accounts of the *CSM*, "de mucha curiosidad, assí por la poesía, como por los trages de aquella edad, que se veen en sus pinturas".

1677

3 Ortiz de Zúñiga, Diego, *Anales eclesiásticos y seculares de la*

15

ciudad de Sevilla (Madrid: Impta Real por Juan García Infançon, 1677).
Here published, presumably for the first time, from the now-lost Lucas Cortés copy, are several of the *CSM*. In Book I, pp. 36-7 and 43-4, *cantigas* 221 and 256 relate illnesses of Fernando III and Beatriz, Alfonso's parents; these are historical and date, respectively, from 1209 and 1227. Book II, pp. 109-23, employs *cantigas* 257, 323, 292, and 324 for what they reveal of Seville's history. For 292 there is a Spanish translation and an explication of each of the twenty-one strophes. This seems to be the first printed commentary on an Alfonsine poem. Z. accepts unquestioningly Pellicer's attribution to Alfonso of the two spurious strophes of the *Querellas* and prints them along with the apocryphal letter from Alfonso to his *cormano*, A. Pérez de Guzmán (II, pp. 123-4).

1684

4   Papebrochio, Daniel, *Acta vitae S. Ferdinandis regis Castellae et Legionis* (Antwerp, 1684). Later rpt. in *Acta sanctorum*, May, vol. VII (Paris and Rome: V. Palmé, 1866), pp. 275-408.
P. borrows from Zúñiga *cantigas* 221 and 256 (the Galician-Portuguese texts only) to illustrate this biography (see pp. 305-6 and 315). One curiosity here is that P. gives his own Latin prose version of both.

1696

5   Antonio, Nicolás, *Bibliotheca hispana sive hispanorum* (Rome, 1696, 2nd ed. is published as *Bibliotheca hispana vetus*, Madrid, 1788). I cite from a facsimile rpt. of the 2nd ed. (Turin: Bottega d'Erasmo, 1963, 2 vols in 1), II, pp. 79-81.
Book VIII, ch. V, paragraphs 191-6 (and the accompanying notes by Francisco Pérez Bayer) deal with Alfonso. He is credited with the verse *Tesoro*, the spurious *Querellas* (citing Pellicer); the *Libro de Alexandre*, and the *CSM*, the metrical variety of which is incompletely assessed in Bayer's notes. It is claimed that Alfonso's personality is clearly imprinted upon the *CSM* but that others undoubtedly contributed to the whole; A. thus opens up the vital authorship question.

1754

6   Velázquez de Velasco, Luis Joseph, *Orígenes de la poesía castellana* (Málaga: En la Oficina de Francisco Martínez de Aguilar, 1754, 2nd ed., 1797), pp. 27, 35, 46-7, and 79-80 (1st ed.).
V. knows of the Toledo MS through Zúñiga's work (1677). The *CSM*

were meant to be sung in church. Much verse in Castilian is attributed to Alfonso, and strophes of the *Alexandre* and the *Querellas* are cited. Mention is made of the use of 4, 5, 6, 8, 12, 13, and 14-syllable lines in the *CSM*. Most of the information is sketchy and second-hand.

1755

7   Burriel, Fr. A.M., *Paleografia española* (Madrid: Impta Joachin Ibarra, 1755, 2nd ed., 1758 [cited]), pp. 71-5.
This work was issued under the name of a colleague of B.'s, P. Esteban Terreros y Pandó, but for the modern attribution to Burriel, see Pedro Sainz y Rodríguez, *El P. Burriel, paleógrafo* (Madrid, 1926). These are the first words describing the appearance of the *CSM* manuscripts, and how the materials were arranged (for the Toledo MS, in this instance). Plate VIII reproduces the beginning of Prol. B and also a *cobla* substituted for another in the margin of *cantiga* 77 (Mettmann 132).

8   Palomares, Francisco Santiago, copyist, "Poesías del Rey don Alonso X".
This is a very faithful manuscript copy (made in Toledo, 1755) of the Toledo MS now in the BN. The copy fills 315 folios and carries several marginal notations by Padre Burriel (reproduced in Anglés, *La música*, 1953, pp. 20-1). This unique copy is BN MS 13055.

1775

9   Sarmiento, Martín, *Memorias para la historia de la poesía y poetas españoles* (Madrid: J. Ibarra, 1775), pp. 268-301.
Actually written in 1741 and published posthumously. S. laments the meager study of Alfonso as poet, having only minor praise for Zúñiga (above, 1677). He corrects his contemporaries in stating that the language of the *CSM* is Galician (Rübecamp, 1933, gives detailed evidence for this view). He has seen the Toledo MS and cites briefly from Prol. A. The remaining few strophes cited are copied from Papebrochio's defective rendering (1684). The then common attribution of the *Alexandre* to Alfonso is rejected, but the poetic *Tesoro* (which is commented at length) and the *Querellas* still remain among Alfonso's attributed works.

1777

10   Ibáñez de Segovia, Gaspar, Marqués de Mondéjar, *Memorias históricas del rei don Alonso el Sabio, i observaciones a su chronica* (Madrid: J. Ibarra, 1777), pp. 436-40, 450-60.
Reviews the devotion of Alfonso to Mary as shown by donations to various sanctuaries and cites discovery of the 1279 *privilegio* chartering the military

Order of Santa María (pp. 438-40). He follows others in ascribing to Alfonso the *Querellas* and also cites an Alexander poem with 6-line strophes. He calls the *CSM* the *Loores* and cites, from the copy seen in Lucas Cortés' library, *cantiga* 324. However, the following account of the contents, meter, etc. of the *CSM* is cursory and oversimplified, leading to error (pp. 457-8).

1779

11   Sánchez, Tomás Antonio, ed., *Colección de poesías castellanas anteriores al siglo XV*, I (Madrid: Por D. Antonio de Sancha, 1779), pp. 96-9, 148-70.
Declares that Alfonso was not the author of the *Alexandre* but that, perhaps, Berceo was (pp. 96-9). S. credits Alfonso with the *Querellas* of about 1282-4 and with the verse *Tesoro* whose verses are printed (pp. 153-60, minus the unintelligible ciphers). S. presents a logic for not accepting the *Tesoro* as authentic but makes no final judgment. He also thinks it likely that Alfonso had Guiraut Riquier draft the Provençal verses attributed to him in the *Declaratio*, an idea now universally accepted.

1782

12   Vargas y Ponce, Joseph, *Elogio del Rey D. Alonso el Sabio.* . Discurso del 15 de octubre, 1782, ante la RAE (Madrid, 1782), 76 pp., esp. pp. 23-4 and 73. Rpt. in the *Memorias de la RAE*, II (1870), 373-432.
Grandiloquent and patriotic in the extreme. The orator notes briefly that Alfonso wrote the *CSM*, the *Alexandre*, and the *Querellas*. The remainder is concentrated on the legal, mathematical and historical genius of Alfonso.

1786

* 13   Quiñones, Hernán, *Elogio de Alfonso X, rey de Castilla y León, llamado el Sabio* (Madrid: P. Barco López, 1786). 95 pp.
An eighteenth-century oration of little interest now except that, agreeing with Mondéjar (1777), Q. believes that Alfonso's poetry was in Castilian! The *Querellas* are specifically attributed to Alfonso (p. LXV).

14   Rodríguez de Castro, D. Joseph, *Biblioteca española*, II (Madrid, 1786), pp. 361-2, 625-43.
Although, as in Pellicer and others, the *Querellas* are still considered Alfonsine, the *Alexandre* is not. Comments on the three codexes are the result of first-hand inspection and are accompanied by *cantigas* 410 and 411, both prologues, 2 and 401 in fairly respectable transcriptions (no punctuation is provided, however). An attempt is made to classify lines according to length: 6, 7, 8, 9, 10, 11, 12, 13, and 16 syllables. R. de

C. regrets that Alfonso's non-Marian poems are lost but does, at least, recognize that Alfonso indeed wrote profane poems.

1797

15　Bosarte, Isidoro, "Reflexiones sobre un punto de literatura y mérito literario del Rey D. Alfonso el Sabio", Academia de la Historia MS 11-3-5, legajo 3 (written in Madrid, 1797).
The misleading "mérito" of the title, rather than truly literary, is Alfonso's use of a new, high-quality kind of paper, *pergamino de paños*.

1806

16.　Pérez Villamil, Juan, *Origen é instituto de la Orden Militar de Santa María de España*. Discurso leído (1806) ante la Acad. de la Hist. Academia de la Historia MS 11-3-5, legajo 1. Published in *BRAH*, LXXIV (1919), 234-52.
Significant as an historical note documenting Alfonso's devotion to the Virgin. P.V. believes the Order was originally meant to be a kind of marine force but was subsumed (1280) into the Order of Santiago after a brief existence.

1821

17.　Clemencín, Diego, "Biblioteca de la Reina: Ilustración XVII", *Memorias de la RAH*, VI (1821), 431-81.
Publishes, from documents in the Simancas archives, a list of Isabel la Católica's books of which no. 132 (p. 457) would appear to be a copy of the *CSM*.

1826

18.　Anon., "Don Alfonso el Sabio. Noticia biográfica y literaria", *Ocios de Españoles Emigrados* (London), V (1826), 84-94.
More a curiosity than anything else. Attributes to Alfonso the *CSM*, the *Querellas*, the poetic *Tesoro*, and the introduction of the use of paper. Written for Spaniards living in London, the article reveals the basic octosyllabic meter of the *Cantigas* (for actual usage, see Kline, 1950), and says that the first strophe only was set to music.

1827

19.　S., V., "Alonso X", *Repertorio Americano* (London), III (1827), 67-77.

Another curious notice in the form of an encyclopedia entry which cites from the *Partidas*, among other things, the ways in which a king may compose music and poetry and reward others for so doing. The *Querellas* and the poetic *Tesoro* are ascribed to Alfonso, as are the *CSM*, though the reference to them cites only the few *cantigas* given by Rodríguez de Castro (1786).

1830

20. Fernández de Moratín, Leandro, *Obras*, I. *Orígenes del teatro español, Parte primera: Discurso histórico* (Madrid: RAH, 1830), pp. 60-1.
   The author attributes both Castilian and Galician poems to Alfonso but explicitly denies paternity for the *Querellas* and for the verse *Tesoro* on the basis that they both betray later literary and linguistic style.

1840

21. Bellermann, Christian Fr., *Die alten Liederbücher der Portugiesischen oder Beiträge zur Geschichte der portugiesischen Poesie vom dreizehnten bis zum Anfang des sechzehnten Jahrhunderts* (Berlin: F. Dümmler, 1840), pp. 15-19.
   The specific section, "Die galizischen Lieder Alfons X", discusses Alfonso and three MSS of the *CSM* (Toledo and the two Escurial MSS). There are excerpts and German translations of the first two strophes of Prol. B (his source was Rodríguez de Castro, 1786), and the complete text of *cantiga* 323 (from Zúñiga, 1677, p. 111), also in German translation.

1846

22 García de Gregorio, Eugenio, "Las *Cantigas* del Rey Sabio", *Siglo Pintoresco*, II (1846), 241-3.
   Contains an early description of the Toledo MS, the earliest "edition" of the *CSM*. Comments are sketchy and general and follow Rodríguez de Castro. The Palomares-Burriel copy (1755) is cited but it remains in doubt that the author had seen the Toledo MS which, as he says, causes so much awe in foreigners.

1849

23 Ticknor, George, *History of Spanish Literature* (New York: Harper & Bros., 1849), I, pp. 39-41.
   T. had done his homework and the commentary reflects his perusal of the earlier criticism. He had the good sense to cast doubt on the authenticity

of the verse *Tesoro* but continues to believe in the authenticity of the *Querellas*. Limited knowledge (derived from Zúñiga and Castro) caused him to overstate the Provençal influence in the *CSM* and to inaccurately gauge their metrical variety.

1852

24   Caveda y Nava, José, "Memoria leída en la Acad. de la Hist. acerca de la empresa de publicar las obras legales y literarias de Don Alfonso el Sabio", *Memorias de la RAH*, VIII (1852), xli.
This speech, as far as I can determine, was never printed in full, though it is cited in various bibliographies.

24 bis (1854) See p. 113.

1855

25   Soriano Fuertes, Mariano, *Historia de la música española desde la venida de los Fenicios hasta el año 1850*, I (Madrid: Martín y Salazar, 1855), pp. 90-100.
This item led to much misunderstanding in its day. Noting that the musical variants between the Toledo MS and the two Escurial MSS are significant, S.F. gives dubious transcriptions of the music of *cantigas* 221, 256, 2, 17, 6 and 28. He attributes the first two to the hand of Fernando III, but a reading of the texts shows this to be absurd. He concedes that Alfonso was not the sole author but posits that many poems were leftovers from an earlier era, collected later. We learn that some of these poems are in Castilian, that MS T.j.l. has 290 poems (it contains 193), and that Alfonso wrote an equal number of profane poems (this deduced from the allusion in Prol. B). This is simply careless scholarship.

25 bis (1856) See pp. 113-14.

1857

26   Gómez de la Serna, Pedro, *Sobre el reinado de Don Alfonso X el Sabio e influencia que ha ejercido en los siglos posteriores*, Discurso de ingreso (13 dic. 1857) ante la Acad. de la Hist. (Madrid: Impta de la *Revista de Legislación*, 1857). 72 pp. (Includes the response of D. Modesto Lafuente).
Disappointing, given the promise of the title. The small note of historical interest is the praise bestowed in the phrase acclaiming Alfonso's poetic talent: the mention of the "de todos sabidas y de nadie olvidadas" *Querellas*. Even worse, historical judgements are based on the two strophes of this apocryphal poem and its supposed circumstances.

1859

27   Wolf, Ferdinand Joseph, *Historia de las literaturas castellana y portuguesa*, trans. from the German original of 1859 by Miguel de Unamuno, with notes by M. Menéndez y Pelayo (Madrid: La España Moderna, 1895), II, pp. 452-73, esp. pp. 467-9.

Most significant because notice is given of the poets of the recently un-covered Portuguese *cancioneiros*, and of Alfonso as a poet of profane, secular lyrics. Wolf agrees with Bellermann (1840) that Alfonso ought to be included, as poet, in the literary history of Galician-Portuguese. Also, there are important doubts cast on both the *Querellas* and the verse *Tesoro* as Alfonsine works.

1861

28   Milá y Fontanals, Manuel, *De los trovadores en España: Estudio de lengua y poesía provenzal* (Barcelona: J. Verdaguer, 1861); 528 pp. 2nd ed., 1889, 558 pp. 3rd ed., ed. C. Martínez and F. R[ico] Manrique, *Obras* de M.M. y F., II (Barcelona: CSIC, 1966), 503 pp.

On pp. 179-218 (3rd ed.) is a lengthy study of Provençal-Catalan poets who paid public (written) homage to Alfonso in their compositions, some alluding to his poetic court with much appreciation. Milá includes Guiraut Riquier's *Declaratio*, a poetical work which is supposed to reflect Alfonso's own thought on classes of poets and poetry. The *CSM* are taken up – with metrics in mind – on pp. 464-8. Brief recognition is given to Alfonso as musician (p. 496).

1862

29   [Morayta de Sagrario, Miguel], "Cantigas de D. Alfonso X", *Revista Ibérica de Ciencias, Política, Literatura, Artes e Instrucción Pública*, IV (1862), 304-10, 468-73.

M. had previously published an appreciation of Alfonso's *CSM* (1856) and now publishes four texts in order to make them more available to a wider public (one of the first such attempts). The four, *cantigas* 63, 64, 42, and 16, are printed without commentary or identifying numbers (I have sup-plied numbers from Mettmann's edition [1959]).

1863

30   Amador de los Ríos, José, *Historia crítica de la literatura española*, III (Madrid: privately publ., ptd J. Rodríguez, 1863;

rpt. Madrid: Gredos, 1969), pp. 499-524.
A. has little of real relevance. However, he was the first to supply truly quotable lines on the literary quality of the *CSM*. He banishes the verse *Tesoro* from the Alfonsine canon because of anachronisms (see also his Appendix III). He compounds the false attribution of the *Querellas* to Alfonso by filling one of their gaps with the *romance* (not by Alfonso) which begins: "Yo salí de mi tierra".

1865

31 Eslava, Hilarión, "Cantiga 14 del rey don Alfonso el Sabio, parafraseada con coros y orquesta por H.E." (Madrid: Fétis, n.d. [*ca* 1865]).
Not seen. Cited by Palau, *Manual*, I, 206. Arraiza (1927) states that E. worked on *cantiga* 15.

31 bis (1866) See p. 114.

31 tris (1870) See p. 114.

1872

32 Ward, Mary, "Alfonso the Wise, King of Castille", *Macmillans Magazine*, XXVI (1872), 126-36. Also in *Littell's Living Age* (Boston), Fourth Series, CXIV (1872), 51-9.
The choice of Galician-Portuguese represents a personal link between Alfonso and the hearer of these songs which the author claims were sung over Alfonso's grave in Toledo for hundreds of years. A narrative genius saves them from severe awkwardness and *cantiga* 94 is given as an example of "fresh simplicity". An English version of the *mayas* (*CSM* 406) is provided. The *Querellas* are given as Alfonsine. There is an attempt at evaluation of Alfonso's literary talent.

1873

33 Cueto, Leopoldo Augusto de, Marqués de Valmar, "Fraternidad de los idiomas y de las letras de Portugal y de Castilla", *MRAE*, IV (1873), 44-141.
Of especial interest are pp. 68-91 in which the author presents some good discussion of the poetic-linguistic situation of the Peninsula. Too facile a credence is lent to Soriano Fuertes (1855) with regard to music. Still, from the future editor (1889) of the *CSM* these are valuable and thoughtful reflections on Alfonso as artist and creator.

34 Valera, Juan, "Las Cantigas del Rey Sabio", *MRAE*, IV (1873),

142-77. Rpt. in *Obras completas*, III (2nd ed., Madrid: Aguilar, 1947), pp. 1115-30.
The Royal Academy requested V. to write this exposition of the *CSM* before its own edition was ready. He may have consulted the MSS but relies heavily on Milá and others. Claims the *CSM* are to Portuguese literature what the *Poema de Mio Cid* is to Castilian. Rambling, prolix, and digressive throughout. It did make better known, at the time of its publication, certain *cantigas*: 103, 3, 122, 283, 84, 54, 135, 128, 208, 104, 148, 155, 188, 196, 153, 162, 72, 141, 312, 55, 67, 38, 238, 255, 215, and 221. V. clearly prefers the narrative poems to the purely lyric *loores* which are disavowed without discussion. Advances the idea that Alfonso was both editor and contributor and that he used diverse sources (reproving, in this aspect, Amador [1863]).

1874

35 Amador de los Ríos, José, "La pintura en pergamino en España hasta fines del siglo XIII (códice de los *Cantares et loores de Sancta María* conocido bajo el título de las *Cántigas* del Rey Sabio)", *Museo Español de Antigüedades*, III (1874), 1-41.
Overlong and exasperatingly repetitious, this study chronicles the story of art on parchment from classic times. A. dates the Alfonsine miniatures at 1275-84, executed in Seville by unknown *mudéjar* artists. This and other pseudo-critical points on artistic techniques (pp. 25-35) come under heavy critical fire in the better work by Guerrero Lovillo (1949, pp. 11-12). Still, the idea of an eclectic group of artists at work on a multiform theatre for presentation of the Virgin's miracles, and the astute deduction – prior to the discovery of the MS in Florence – that the Lucas Cortés copy of the *CSM*, seen by most of the earlier critics, must have been a complement to Escurial T.j.l., are two examples of the kind of intuitional judgements for which we have to be grateful to A.

1875

36 C., J., "Alfonso the Wise", *Fraser's Magazine*, New Series, XII (1875), 627-39.
A curiosity. Scant mention of the *Cantiguos* [sic], but it will interest those who follow the history of the apocryphal legends and poems associated with Alfonso, for all of them are taken quite seriously.

37 Monaci, Ernesto, *Il canzoniere portoghese della Biblioteca Vaticana* (Halle: Max Niemeyer, 1875), 456 pp. + 2 facs.
A diplomatic edition of Vatican MS 4803, which contains nineteen of Alfonso's *cantigas profanas* (*CV* 61-79). It is less useful than Braga's

(1878) but is more faithful. The history and description of the MS, in the introduction, is thorough. I have not seen the selection from *CV* said to have been published in 1873 under the title *Canti antiche.*

1877

38 Salas, Francisco Javier de, "Hallazgo de la nave y galera del siglo XIII, en el notable Códice de las *Cantigas*", *Museo Español de Antigüedades*, VI (1877), 47-58.
Despite the title, this is a small history of boats through the ages. The *CSM* are mentioned because the nine illustrations the author has seen from T.j.l., if they are accurately drawn, are not in conformity with the textual references from the period. A final decision is left to the better qualified.

1878

39 Braga, Theófilo, *Cancioneiro portuguez da Vaticana. Edição crítica, restituida sobre o texto diplomático de Halle, acompanhada de um glossário e de uma introducção sobre os trovadores e cancioneiros portuguezes* (Lisbon: Imprensa Nacional, 1878). 236 pp.
A more accessible and readable text than Monaci's (1875). A new edition is very much needed, however, to take into account the contributions of critics such as C. Michaëlis de Vasconcellos, J.J. Nunes, J. Piel, W. Mettmann and others. Alfonso's poems are numbered 61-79 and appear on pp. 12-17, but B. attributes them to Alfonso IX (d. 1229).

1880

40 Molteni, Enrico Gasi, *Il canzoniere portoghese (Colocci-Brancuti) pubblicato nelle parti che completano il codice Vaticano 4.803* (Halle: Max Niemeyer, 1880). 187 pp. + 1 facs.
The *Colocci-Brancuti* (*CB*) is a vast collection and is now housed in Lisbon's Biblioteca Nacional. Here M. published, in a diplomatic edition, only those poems not included in the *CV* which Monaci published in 1875. Of these there are twenty-six by Alfonso (nos 348-72) and one *tenson* by Alfonso and Vaasco Gil (no. 385). *CB* 359 is also *CSM* 40 and the beginning of *CB* 360 is a fragment of a *loor* not included in the *CSM*. For the corresponding numbers in various editions of Alfonso's satirical and love songs, see Appendix A.

40 bis (1881)   See pp. 114-15.

1885

41 Fita, Fidel, "Cincuenta leyendas por Gil de Zamora, combinadas

con las *Cantigas* de Alfonso el Sabio", *BRAH*, VII (1885),
54-141.
For most of the fifty Latin prose legends by Gil de Zamora we have Fita's
helpful notes. The fifty corresponding *CSM* accounts are *cantigas* 2-4, 7,
11-14, 19, 21, 23-7, 29, 32-4, 36-7, 39, 41, 45, 47, 49, 51, 53, 54, 61-3,
66-7, 73, 81, 86-7, 101, 106, 111, 125, 132, 139, 216, 254, 255, 298, 308,
and 15. Gil's work is dated *ca* 1280, too late to be a source for Alfonso,
and F. concludes that Gil de Zamora rejected Alfonso as a source for his
own rather more historical compilation.

42   ——, "Variantes de tres leyendas por Gil de Zamora", *BRAH*,
VI (1885), 418-29.
F., as is his wont, prints the texts with barebones notes only. For scholars
tracing sources and (Latin) analogues, texts for comparison with *CSM* 87,
132, 125, 111, 11, and 36 are provided.

1886

43   ——, "La judería de Segovia", *BRAH*, IX (1886), 270-93, 344-
89, and 460-9.
Section 9, "Marisaltos ó la hebrea de la Fuencisla: Siglo XIII (pp. 372-89)",
treats the events recorded in *CSM* 107. F. accepts the witness of the un-
edited XIII-cent. MS of Rodrigo, *el Cerratense*, and firmly places these
events in 1237. The remainder of the art. deals with the ulterior development of the deed, as fact and as legend, in succeeding centuries.

1887

44   De Lollis, Cesare, "*Cantigas de amor e de maldezir* di Alfonso el
Sabio", *Studi di Filologia Romanza*, II (1887), 31-66.
De L. disputes the claims of Braga (1878) that the poems of *CV*, 61-79,
belong to Alfonso IX (d. 1229). With an arsenal of logic, he reconstructs
the events and personages alluded to, and convincingly demonstrates (as
none before had bothered to do) the authorship of these poems, as well
as those of *CB* 467-96, to be that of Alfonso X. Alfonso VIII is also elimi-
nated as a prospective author. This is the study that first established these
data and the scholarship involved is first-rate.

45   Riaño, Juan F., *Critical and Bibliographical Notes on Early
Spanish Music* (London: Quaritch, 1887; rpt. N.Y.: DaCapo
Press, 1971).
Chapter 8, on the "*CSM*, attributed to the King Don Alonso el Sabio",
surveys work leading up to the 1889 edition. It tells us that the well-known
musicologist, Barbieri, was transcribing the music for the Academy, a fact
made more interesting when one ponders the inspiration provided for

Ribera (1921, 1922) by this same Barbieri.

46 Teza, Emilio, "Trifoglio. Un viaggio fantastico, in portoghese – Dal canzoniere francese di Siena – Dalle cantiche di Alfonso X", *ZRP*, XI (1887), 289-304, esp. 301-4.

An early and exact, almost diplomatic, rendering of *cantiga* 408 ("Despirital cilurgia") and of 309 ("Non deven por maravilla") from the Florence MS, whose variants were not used by Valmar in his 1889 edition of the *CSM*. T. calls Alfonso a pious writer with a meagre poetic gift.

1888

47 Fita, Fidel, "San Dunstán, arzobispo de Cantorbery, en una cantiga del Rey D. Alfonso el Sabio", *BRAH*, XII (1888), 244-8.

Citing a contemporary biography of St Dunstan (d. 988) and contrasting it with the narration of *CSM* 288 and the Gil de Zamora account (*Liber Mariae*, tractatus VII), F. allows that the English account reached the latter via the intermediary chronicle of the monk of Montfroid, Hélinand (*ca* 1204). All texts are quoted. In addition, F. believes that there may be a source for *cantiga* 23 in the Dunstan biography as well.

48 ——, "Treinta leyendas por Gil de Zamora", *BRAH*, XIII (1888), 187-225.

These complement the fifty previously published by Fita (1885). No. 56 is related to *CSM* 288; others, especially those dealing with Soissons (for example, Gil de Zamora's 71 and *CSM* 101) seem to warrant further study. Unlike the earlier study, this one does not give much information on similarities between Gil's work and Alfonso's.

1889

49 Cueto, Leopoldo Augusto de, Marqués de Valmar, ed., *Las 'Cantigas de Santa Maria' de Alfonso el Sabio*, 2 vols (Madrid: RAE, 1889). Part of the first vol. was issued separately, in a smaller format, as *Estudio histórico, crítico y filosófico sobre las 'Cantigas' del Rey D. Alfonso el Sabio* (Madrid: ptd Tip. de Sucesores de Rivadeneyra, 1897). 395 pp.

Many years in preparation, the Academy edition, prepared by Valmar with the assistance of many others, is the true beginning of modern scholarship on the *CSM* (excepting the music, for which see Ribera, 1922). The transcription is of Escurial MS J.b.2: it occupies the latter part of vol. I and the bulk of vol. II and is paginated continuously despite this break. Variants are noted from the Toledo codex (now in the BN) and from Escurial T.j.1, but not from the Florence MS, which had only recently been reported (see Teza, 1887). There are some colour plates dispersed throughout, and vol. II ends with a vast glossary which is occasionally inaccurate. Vol. I contains eight chapters of study on various aspects of the *cantigas*: prior history of *CSM* scholarship; the codices; themes; sources; Alfonso and his era; language of the *CSM*; versification; and, finally, the character and personality of the poet-monarch Alfonso. These chapters, especially 1, 2, 4, and 5, offer very interesting reading, in particular for their able defense of Alfonso as a poet of no small literary worth. The scholarship, given its distance in time from us and the tools with which it had to create this achievement, is very solid indeed, and it is still the point of departure for all serious modern studies, many of which have modified Valmar's judgments slightly. Less successful are, I think, the chapters on themes, versification and Alfonso's character. They are vague and tentative, but should be read (one digression in chapter 8 — on Dante's disapproval of Alfonso — is fascinating, even if it is not, as V. supposed, Alfonso X to whom Dante makes reference).

Following these chapters there is a section with Castilian prose summaries of the *CSM* (cxxviii pp.). These are thematically arranged and have very useful bibliographical notes on the locations of analogous legends and tales (supplied by P. Meyer, A. Mussafia, T. Braga, F. Fita, E. Monaci, E. Teza, and A. D'Ancona, *inter alios*). The editing of the text is very conservative, apart from liberal use of accents. It served well until Anglés (1943) and, most importantly, Mettmann (1959-64) edited the *CSM* anew.

50   Fita, Fidel, "La cantiga LXIX del Rey D. Alfonso el Sabio. Fuentes históricas", *BRAH*, XV (1889), 179-91.

F. prints *cantiga* 69 and his own Castilian translation of it. The main thrust is in the corroborating historical docs, also published here, which show that the miracle, confirmed for April of 1150, was used as part of a propaganda campaign to support the substitution of the Roman rite for the Mozarabic, especially in Toledo.

1892

51   Blake, Mary E., "Alonso X and the Birth of Spanish Literature", *Catholic World*, LVI (1892-3), 518-30.

A popularizing art. of no profundity. B. paints a black portrait of *King Alonso* and a much brighter one of Alonso *el Sabio*. The comments on the *CSM* are limited but fairly accurate (pp. 522-5). Follows Valera (1873) in preferring the narrative parables to the lyric *loores*. There is a partial translation of *cantiga* 79 — the tale of Musa — and a few other *CSM* are mentioned. Attributes the rhymed *Tesoro* to Alfonso and gives a sample of it through Longfellow's English trans.

52 Monaci, Ernesto, "Le *Cantigas* di Alfonso el Sabio", *Rendiconti della Reale Accademia dei Lincei (Classe de Scienze Morali, Storiche e Filologiche)*, Series V, I (1892), 3-18.
A non-critical review of Valmar's edition (1889), with a summary of his opinions. Begins with a panegyric of Alfonso's civilizing contributions and attempts to evoke, using the miniatures of the *CSM* MSS, the vast cultural enterprise of his court. A poetically-written essay, rather good of its kind.

1893

53 Durrieu, Paul, "Manuscrits d'Espagne remarquables par leur peintures . . . à la Biblioteca Nacional et à la Bibliothèque de l'Escurial", *Bibliothèque de l'École des Chartes*, LIV (1893), 251-326.
A report of what D. has seen in Spain includes high praise for T.j.l. and its miniatures, in which one may recapture vividly both Muslim and Christian Spain on parade.

1895

54 Menéndez y Pelayo, Marcelino, "Las *Cantigas* del Rey Sabio", *La Ilustración Española y Americana*, XXXIX (1895), 127-31, 143-6, and 159-63. Rpt. in *Obras completas, Estudios y discursos de crítica histórica y literaria*, I (Madrid: CSIC, 1941), pp. 161-89.
In what MMP terms the first public review of the Academy edition of the *CSM*, he manages to describe the prior history of these poems briefly and accurately. The discussion, occupying the first third of the critical evaluation, is a fine picture of the situation and influence of Galician in the context of other literary idioms of the times of Alfonso. Unhesitatingly, he declares Alfonso to be sole author of this "Biblia estética del siglo XIII". The final part is a subtle appreciation of Valmar's work, including cavils about cost, lack of accessibility (only 300 were printed), and size (too unwieldy).

55 Mussafia, Adolfo, *Sull'antica metrica portoghese* (Akademie der Wissenschaften, Sitzungsberichte der Philosophisch-Historische Classe, CXXXIII, Abhandlung 10, Vienna, 1895). 36 pp.
Utilizing the poems of Alfonso, esp. *CSM* 282, 21, 70, 60, and 115 (and others by King Dinis of Portugal), M. shows that isosyllabic lines in corresponding positions in successive stanzas were acceptable Galician-Portuguese practice, even though this permits the equation of masculine and feminine lines, and thus departs from the more inflexible French-Provençal system which counts syllables only up to the final stressed one in the line. For the poems adduced, M. proves his case rather well. However, he is forced to

accept that poems with unrhymed lines, whether masculine or feminine in stress, often scan better when the unrhymed lines are conceived of as hemistichs of a longer line. Not only do they scan better, but they then show their isosyllabic nature more clearly. This manner of arranging the poems (not done in the MSS) has been adopted, in the main, with Mettmann's ed. (1959). Mussafia avoids any consideration of compositions which are polymetric as they are not pertinent to his topic. One leaves this study feeling that much more needs to be said.

1896

56 Fita, Fidel, "Nueva ilustración a la cantiga LXIII de Alfonso el Sabio", *BRAH*, XXVIII (1896), 261-3.
F. briefly develops the historical basis of *CSM* 63 from accounts contemporaneous with Alfonso, and from surviving records through the nineteenth century.

57 Michaëlis de Vasconcellos, Carolina, "Randglossen zum altportugiesischen Liederbuch", *ZRP*, XX (1896), 145-218; XXV (1901), 129-74, 278-321, 533-60, and 669-85; XXVI (1902), 56-75, 206-29; XXVII (1903), 153-72, 257-77, 414-36, and 708-37; XXVIII (1904), 385-434; and XXIX (1905), 683-711.
A compendious 426-page, fifteen-part study of great value for its acute historical, lexicographical, and comparative notes on the *cancioneiros* and, in particular, the satirical poems. All sections but the last contain notes relevant to Alfonso, his poems, poems in which he appears, or poets with whom he had frequent contact. There is no index. The following pages are the most important for Alfonsine items: 1896, pp. 208-9 (for *CB* 461/353); 1901, pp. 278-96 (for *CV* 63, 69, 74, 77, and 79), pp. 533 ff., esp. 547 (for *CV* 78), pp. 669-70 (*CV* 64); 1902, p. 227 (*CSM* 223), pp. 165-72 (*CSM* 345); and 1904, pp. 421-6, 429-31 (*CSM* 274 and *CB* 358, respectively). Other references *passim* in text and notes.

1897

58 Martínez Salazar, A., "La Edad Media en Galicia: Una gallega célebre en el siglo XIII", *Revista Crítica de Historia y Literatura Españolas, Portuguesas e Hispano-Americanas*, II (1897), 298-304.
The author has come upon a doc. of 1257 in which a María Pérez figures prominently, and he identifies her with the famous Maria Balteira of Alfonso's *CV* 64. Since the evidence of the doc. conflicts with the many poetic testimonies, the author offers the weak conclusion that the poems are envious and jealous descriptions of an otherwise pious woman.

59 Michaëlis de Vasconcellos, Carolina, and Theófilo Braga,

"Geschichte der portugiesische Litteratur", in *Grundriss der romanischen Philologie*, ed. Gustav Gröber, II (Strasbourg: K.J. Trübner, 1897), pp. 178-86.
These few pages pull together much of what was known of Alfonso's poetic court and the personal poetic efforts of the king. Both are tied to his early experiences with the Galician idiom, to which Alfonso wedded some troubadour adornments (especially in the area of metrical combinations) as he fashioned his *CSM*. Especially praised are *CSM* 421 (Mettmann 406), the *mayas*, the *alba* (*cantiga* 340), and the *loor* akin to the *Salve regina* (*cantiga* 40).

1898

60 Cotarelo y Mori, Emilio, "Sobre el supuesto libro de las *Querellas* del Rey D. Alfonso el Sabio", *Revista Contempóranea*, CX (1898), 113-35. Rpt. in *Estudios de historia literaria de España* (Madrid: Impta de la *Revista Española*, 1901), pp. 5-31.
A wonderfully detailed detective study of two works attributed to Alfonso: the strophes of the *Querellas* which Pellicer first brought to light (1663) and also the ballad, "Yo salí de mi tierra". Although neither can be assigned to Alfonso any longer (especially after this study) Cotarelo's search is fascinating, complete with a surprise twist as to the identity of the perpetrator of the original hoax.

61 Fitzmaurice-Kelly, James, *A History of Spanish Literature* (London: William Heinemann and N.Y.: D. Appleton, 1898, rpt. 1907, 1915, and 1918). Expanded as *A New History of Spanish Literature* (London: Humphrey Milford, Oxford University Press, 1926; rpt. N.Y.: Russell and Russell, 1968).
Alfonso found his métier in Galician and, if not a great poet, he outperformed his predecessors. He had the brain of a giant and the heart of a child and was the writer of "brutally erotic and satiric verse" (1898 ed., pp. 69-71). He was only part author, given to variations on a theme and metrical experimentation and such games as acrostics (*New History*, pp. 30-31).

1899 (?)

62 Anon., *Extractos de las Cantigas de Santa Maria en lengua castellana.*
A strange volume, without date or name of editor. The extracts are divided into groups and numbered according to MS J.b.2. For example, group I is "Leyendas curiosas, algunas de índole especial" and contains a prose summary of *cantiga* 4, among others. The final group is the *loores*,

of which only the merest indication is given, as extracts of lyrics are very difficult to produce. Poem 400 ends this volume abruptly. Pages are printed on the right-hand side only. The book seems to date from the latter part of the nineteenth century. A copy (possibly unique), which once belonged to Pascual de Gayangos, is in the BN of Madrid and carries the shelf-mark: 1/18470.

1900 (?)

63   Villalba Muñoz, P. Luis, *Cántigas a la Inmaculada Virgen María: Cántiga X de el rey D. Alfonso el Sabio, armonizada por el P.L.V.* (Madrid: Ildefonso Alier, 190?), 4 pp.

CSM 10 arranged for unison chorus. These sheet music pages contain the entire text and the original music from MS J.b.2. The Spanish lyrics, a translation, are by P.R. del Valle. The tempo is slightly faster than in Anglés's 1943 transcription of the same *cantiga.*

1901

64   De Lollis, Cesare, "Per una canzone di Alfonso X", *Studi di Filologia Romanza*, no. 8 (1901), 380-6.

While noting the absurdity of the attribution of the late *romance*, "Yo salí de mi tierra," to Alfonso, De L. calls attention to a thematic similarity of its last stanza (seeking comfort in the sea) to *CV* 63 which is genuinely Alfonsine. The latter text is given, with a tentative explication of its symbolic meanings.

65   Hanssen, Friedrich, "Los versos de las *CSM* del rey Alfonso X", *AUCh*, CVIII (1901), 338-73, 501-46.

In terms of either their metrical length or their rhythms, nearly all of the *CSM* are highlighted in this detailed and generously illustrated discussion. Technical terminology requires close concentration but the art. is successful. A listing of verse types at the end of the second part (pp. 542-6) is constructed according to rhythmic patterns and selects a representative *cantiga* for each.

66   Serrano Fatigati, Enrique, *Instrumentos músicos en las miniaturas de los códices españoles (X-XIII)*, Discursos leídos ante la Real Academia de Bellas Artes de San Fernando (Madrid, 1901). 30 pp.

Often cited, this pamphlet is neither overly detailed nor particularly helpful. There is a general description and classification of instruments, with a few notes on their construction and materials used in the manufacture of each. One of the main sources for illuminations, of course, is MS J.b.2 of the Escurial Library.

1903

67   Hanssen, Friedrich, *Metrische Studien zu Alfonso und Berceo* (Valparaiso and Santiago: Impta Guillermo Helfmann, 1903). 36 pp.
An offprint from vol. V of the Verhandlungen des Deutschen Wissenschaftlichen Vereines zu Santiago which I have not seen. Pages 1-22 treat Alfonso, the rest Berceo. The survey of the *CSM* deals with iambs, trochees, anapests, dactyls, both masculine and feminine endings, long and short lines, and types of verse and metrical combinations. The conclusion is that Alfonso is closer to Latin hymnody than to traditional Spanish prosodic patterns.

1904

68   Cotarelo y Valledor, Armando, *Una cantiga célebre del Rey Sabio. Fuentes y desarrollo de la leyenda de Sor Beatriz, principalmente en la literatura española.* (Madrid: Impta de Antonio Marzo, 1904). 205 pp.
Title is rather misleading. The *cantiga* in question − *CSM* 94 − is more a point of departure. The general theme, later treated by Lope and Zorrilla, has three examples in Alfonso's work: *CSM* 55, 94, and 285. Each has a French original, respectively an adaptation of Caesarius von Heisterbach, an account by Gautier de Coincy, and a selection from the *Vie des pères*. Similar and/or parallel themes are encountered in *CSM* 58, 59, 63, and 216 (pp. 37-60). Noteworthy more for its breadth than its depth.

69   Michaëlis de Vasconcellos, Carolina, ed. *Cancioneiro de Ajuda*, 2 vols (Halle: Max Niemeyer, 1904).
None of the Ajuda texts is by Alfonso. However, vol. II, pp. 61-8, contains some observations on earlier appreciations of Alfonso's poetry in other *cancioneiros*, e.g., De Lollis (1887), Valmar (1889), and Menéndez y Pelayo (1895), and a lengthy discussion of the poetic interplay between Alfonso, Pero da Ponte, and Bernaldo de Bonaval (pp. 457-64). See also Index (II, p. 951) for other Alfonsine references.

1905

70   Leite de Vasconcellos, José, "Santa Maria de Terena no século XIII", *O Archeólogo Português*, X (1905), 340-3.
The author mentions twelve of the *CSM* as taking place at the Portuguese sanctuary of Terena, now non-existent (he omits a thirteenth, *cantiga* 223). He describes the geographical setting and the cult practised there, and concludes that Alfonso knew the area personally and that Marian worship there had overtones of a pre-existing pagan goddess cult.

71   Pedrell, Felipe, *Seis cantigas, transcriptas y harmonizadas con acompañamiento de órgano o harmonio. Textos originales y versiones en castellano* (Barcelona: Vidal Llimona y Boceta, ¿1905-191??).
Uncommented sheet music for unison chorus and solo voice for *CSM* 28, 60, 61, 65, 200, and 230. A separate voice part is inserted for *cantiga* 28. These probably appeared first, singly, in the review, *Salterio Sacro Hispano, ca* 1882-3, which Pedrell founded. The transcriptions are among the first modern ones attempted and later researches have shown them to be flawed (see especially Anglés, 1943).

71 bis (1905)   See p. 115.

1906

72   Aubry, Pierre, "Les *CSM* de don Alfonso el Sabio", *Sammelbände der Internationalen Musik-Gesellschaft,* parts I and II published in the 1906-7 vol., and parts III, IV, and V in 1907-8. Also published together as an 84-page monograph (Leipzig, 1908). I cite from its appearance in the author's *Iter Hispanicum. Notices et extraits de manuscrits de musique ancienne conservés dans les bibliothèques d'Espagne* (Paris: Paul Guenther, 1908). 84 pp.
An attempt to assess the musical notation of the *CSM*, a task not taken up by the Academy ed. of 1889. Comparing the unique notation of the music in the Toledo MS with that of the two at the Escurial, A. perceives a development in the use of rhythmic modes in the thirteenth century. He finds the musical construction markedly Iberian, representing a higher degree of sophistication than in the common Gallic form then in wide use elsewhere. He adapts the music of *CSM* 10, 32, 34, 77, 100, 119, 124, 231 and 425, either wholly or in part, but also prints the MS versions so that comparison can be made. Not the last word, but a good first one.

73   Nunes, J.J., *Crestomatia arcaica: excertos da literatura portuguesa, desde o que mais antigo se conhece até ao século XVI* (Lisbon: Livraria Clássica Editora, 1906, 7th ed, 1970). cxxii + 621 pp.
Available here in decent shape (some editorial intervention allowed for) are *CSM* 2, 78, 103, 256, and *CB* 362. There is a linguistic introd. of no small value, some notes, and an acceptable glossary.

1907

74   Fournier d'Albe, Edmond, *Les Miracles de Notre-Dame de Roc-*

Amadour au XIIe siècle. Texte et traduction d'après les manuscrits de la Bibliothèque Nationale (Paris: H. Champion, 1907). MSS 12593, 16565, and 17491 from the Bib. Nat. (Paris) provide 126 miracles associated with Rocamadour in France. Eight similar accounts appear in the *CSM*: 8, 147, 153, 157, 158, 159, 214, and 343. Useful item for students of sources of Alfonsine poetry.

75   Menéndez Pidal, Juan, "Noticias acerca de la Orden Militar de Santa María de España, instituida por Alfonso X", *RABM*, XVI (1907), 161-80.

Alfonso established this Order in 1272 "a serviço de Dios e a loor de la virgen sancta Maria su madre". It was powerful for about ten years (corresponding to the latter additions to the *CSM*) and helps document Alfonso's devotion, in life as well as in literature, to the Virgin. The article relies on the MS of Pérez Villamil's Academy speech (1806).

1908

76   Nobiling, Oskar, "As cantigas de Garcia de Guilhade, trovador", *RF*, XXV (1908), 641-719.

N. makes use of Valmar's ed. of the *CSM* and its glossary in his notes to Guilhade's poetry. Compares usage, meaning, and morphological features, and is one of the first studies to do so.

1909

77   Cabello, Juan, "Alcanate o Santa María del Puerto y el Rey Sabio", *Revista Portuense* (Sept. 11, 1909), no pages cited.

Unlocated item: see Martínez Alfonso (1962).

78   Macías y García, Marcelo, "Las cantigas de la Virgen y el país del Bierzo en la época trovadoresca".

I have seen this cited often but never with enough details to locate it. It is, apparently, an address delivered and published in La Coruña, 1909.

1911

79   Collet, Henri, and Luis Villalba, "Contribution à l'étude des *Cantigas* d'Alphonse le Savant d'après les codices de l'Escurial", *BH*, XIII (1911), 270-90.

A tripartite analysis – thematic, melodic, and rhythmic – of twelve of the *CSM*: 10, 40, 139, 270, 340, 38, 100, 119, 124, 176, 186, and 189. The authors call for more flexibility of musical interpretation than their predecessor Aubry (1906). They admit that, musically speaking, Alfonso is not the composer of all of the *CSM*, and offer solid reasons for their opinion (for more on this, see Anglés, 1943, 1958). This study shows that the original contribution of the music of the *CSM* is the use of the musical refrain in a thematic manner. There is much evidence for the inclusion of local, popular melodies, and even the notation seems to be particularly Peninsular. In their small sample, the authors realize that words and music do not always blend harmoniously and that, in certain cases at least, it is possible to tell which preceded and gave shape to the other. These are very serious considerations confirmed in more detail by later studies in music and in versification of the *CSM*.

80   Michaëlis de Vasconcellos, Carolina, "Mestre Giraldo e os seus Tratados de Alveitaria e Cetraria", *Revista Lusitana*, XIII (1910 [1911]), 149-432. Rpt. in *Dispersos originais portugueses*, II: *Lingüística* (Lisbon: Ed. da *Revista de Portugal*, 1959), 191-429, esp. 231-44.
      Not an easy work to use. The main part of the study is not germane to Alfonso's poetry. Appendix I gathers together *CSM* 44, 142, 232, 242, 352, and 366 as witness to Alfonso's interest in hunting and hawking. Additionally the long etymological glossary often cites from them for support and demonstration of points the author makes in commenting her text, illuminating meanings and contexts found in Alfonso's poems.

1912

81   Sentenach, Narciso, "Los grandes retratistas en España", *Boletín de la Sociedad Española de Excursiones*, XX (1912), 9.
      Reproduces the miniature from MS J.b.2. which, he claims, depicts Alfonso and his literary court. Is this a portrait of Alfonso or is it a stylized depiction of a medieval king?

1913

82   Hanssen, Friedrich, "Los alejandrinos de Alfonso X", *AUCh*, CXXXIII (1913), 81-114.
      A lengthy disquisition on those *cantigas* containing alexandrines, whether alone or in combination with other meters. Most are anapestic and a few are iambic; other types are represented. H. gives examples of all types, accompanied by a schema of the basic metrical rhythm, one stanza from the selected text, and the musical rhythm as found in and interpreted from MS J.b.2. The interpretation, too often, is only approximate and diminishes the utility of the comparisons made. Patterns are presented for the following *cantigas*: 71, 270, 47, 149, 169, 241, 380, 90, 210, 115, 220, 50, 182, 320, 260, 60, 401, 368, 296, 251, 148, 218, 261, 284, 315, 372, FM 1 (411), FM 9 (419), FM 10 (420), 246, 293, 379, and 264.

Rhythmic values of all the substitutions for the anapest are given as well.

83 ——, "Los endecasílabos de Alfonso X: Estudio sobre las *Cantigas*", *BH*, XV (1913), 284-99.
An advance over his study of metrics in Alfonso and Berceo (1903), for now H. more unhesitatingly concludes that the musical notation provides important rhythmic information for a correct interpretation of the individual *cantigas*. For the hendecasyllable as seen in, for example, *CSM* 17, both the grammatical and the musical accents tend to coincide in a dactylic form. H.'s expositions are not always clear to the layman, a fact compounded by the inexpert state of musicological studies of the *CSM* at this time. Schema are provided for: *CSM* 410, 290, 52, 339, 279, 126, 259, 39, 367, 133, 211, 139, 150, 69, 10, 143, 41, and 57. H. claims that these are all anticipated by occurrences in Latin hymnody.

1914

84 ——, "Die jambischen Metra Alfons des X [sic]", *MLN*, XXIX (1914), 65-8.
Brief exposition of iambs in the *CSM*, their varieties and irregularities, and their combinations with other measures. H. depends on the French syllable-counting method in his discussion of meters and is interested, here, in making frequent note of the divergence in musical and grammatical accents.

85 López Aydillo, Eugenio, *Las mejores poesías gallegas* (Madrid: Imprenta Artística Española, 1914), pp. 32-7.
The introduction is, for the time it was printed, very satisfactory. The poems of Alfonso printed are: *CSM* 10, 140, and 70; *CV* 73, 77, 79, and 74.

1915

86 Arco, Ricardo del, "La fama del santuario de Salas en lo antiguo", *Linages de la Corona de Aragón*, VI (1915), 332-7.
Alfonso celebrated seventeen miraculous events connected with Salas in Huesca, and these are part of the "fama" discussed by A. The author seems unaware that Valmar attributed these same miracles to a Salas in Lérida. Only four of the group are cited and incompletely: 52 (occurs in Aragon but Salas is not mentioned), 56, 58, and 163 (A. incorrectly gives 162 as the number). See also Aguado Bleye (1916) and Gili (1921).

87 Bell, Aubrey F.G., "The *CSM* of Alfonso X", *MLR*, X (1915), 338-48.
A rapid summary of the variety of the *CSM*. Lengthy mentions of Alfonso's source-identification formulas, personal and realistic details, and the observation of a certain popular thread that obtains throughout. Some verses

are wooden, although Alfonso was a "zealous and talented *translator*" (my italics). A general, once-over-lightly appraisal.

88   Carré Aldao, Eugenio, *Influencia de la literatura gallega en la castellana: Estudios críticos y bibliográficos* (Madrid: F. Beltrán, 1915), pp. 171-202.
Relies heavily on Valmar's commentaries (1889), but the bibliography was very good in its day. Central focus is on the personal nature of the *CSM* and on the role of Provençal poetry in shaping much of its style. On pp. 193-4 there is a useful listing of the codices of the *CSM* which have been previously cited and which now must be termed lost.

89   Ruiz de Obregón Retortillo, Juan, "Alfonso X, el emplazado: Una leyenda", *RABM*, XXXII (1915), 420-49.
A fairly exhaustive presentation, with a new *inédito*, of the early literature which attributed to Alfonso the blasphemy: "Si yo estuviera con Dios cuando formó el mundo y todas las cosas que en él son, muchas menguas que se hicieron no se hubieran hecho".

90   Solalinde, Antonio G., "Intervención de Alfonso X en la redacción de sus obras", *RFE*, II (1915), 283-8.
Brings to light the now-famous passage from the *General estoria* (Part One, book XVI, ch. xiv) which supports convincingly the notion of Alfonso's direct participation in works bearing his royal rubric. Previous scholarship is generously recognized in the notes.

1916

91   Aguado Bleye, Pedro, *Santa María de Salas en el siglo XIII: Estudio sobre algunas cantigas de Alfonso el Sabio* (Bilbao: Garmendía, 1916). 99 pp. + 2 plates.
A version of the author's doctoral diss. Divided into two parts, a 38-pp. study and 53 pp. of documents. Assigns correctly to Huesca the seventeen Salas miracles Valmar had assigned to Lérida. These miracles are: *CSM* 43, 44, 109, 114, 118, 129, 161, 163, 164, 166, 167, 168, 171, 172, 173, 189, and 247. Singled out for especial treatment is 164 which, when seen in light of documents Aguado presents, is historically accurate as to its people and geographical disposition. This is a valuable study.

1917

92   Barreda, Fr. Íñigo de, *Oña y su real monasterio según la descripción . . . hecha en 1771*, introd. y notas históricas y artísticas por el P. Enrique Herrera y Oña. (Madrid: Tip. de la *Revista de Archivos*, 1917).

Barreda related the tale of Fernando III's miraculous cure at Oña (pp. 133-44) which is the subject of *CSM* 221 (text taken from Papebrochio, 1684). The modern editor substitutes the Valmar text but retains the Latin trans. given by Papebrochio. This has only minor historical interest now.

93   Marden, Charles Carroll, ed., *Libro de Apolonio*, I (Elliott Monographs in Romance Languages and Literatures, VI, Baltimore: Johns Hopkins Univ. Press, 1917), pp. xxxv-xxxvii.
M. outlines the history of the false attribution to Alfonso of the *romance* "Yo salí de mi tierra" from 1524 through the late nineteenth century and Menéndez y Pelayo's *Antología de poetas líricos*, XII, pp. 93-8.

1918

94   Levi, Ezio, "I miracoli della Vergine nell'Arte del Medio Evo", *Bollettino d'Arte*, XII (1918), 1-25.
L. adopts Valmar's position that the art of illumination of the MSS of the *CSM* is of the French school. *Cantiga* 115 is mentioned (p. 7) along with four other accounts of the same tale, in French and Latin. Perhaps this has only limited use for some searching of sources or for comparisons of style and individual treatment, but it is a beginning for this *cantiga*.

95   López Aydillo, Eugenio, and S. Rivera Manescau, "Una cantiga desconocida del Rey Santo", *Revista Histórica*, I (1918), 5-39, 65-72.
The poem, in Galician, written in an earlier thirteenth-century hand and accompanied by a marginal note attributing it to "mi señor D. Fernando, rey de Castilla," is transcribed and edited by the authors. The rhyme scheme, the 9-line stanza, the distinctiveness of its form in contrast to any of Alfonso's forty-one *loores* (to which genre of lyric this poem belongs), all seem to indicate that Alfonso may have had a model for his Marian songs from within his family. Interesting though this may seem, more work will have to be done on this text before any definitive conclusion can be reached.

96   Pedrell, Felipe, *Cancionero musical popular español*, I (Barcelona: Casa Editorial de Música Boileau, 1918), pp. 96-100 (text), 133-6 (examples); 3rd ed. (1958), pp. 104-8 (text), 133-6 (examples).
P's own harmonizations of the refrains from *CSM* 221 and 256 and the refrains and melodies of 60 and 28. Records the anecdote of his meeting with Pierre Aubry and the repercussion of the encounter in Aubry's *Iter Hispanicum* (see 1906).

97   Solalinde, Antonio G., "El códice florentino de las *Cantigas* y su relación con los demás manuscritos", *RFE*, V (1918), 143-79.

A painstaking account of the Florence MS (thirteenth century): the miniatures, the calligraphy, the binding, the contents – in the form of an index – and inclusion of occasional variants noted from MS J.b.2. Two of the *cantigas* (*F* 14 and *F* 86) are unique in this codex and they are printed in full with two black and white plates of *F* 14 (Mettmann 408; the other – *F* 86 – is Mettmann 409) which show both the text and the accompanying miniatures. Two others, corresponding to *CSM* 246 and 209, are also included. Finally, listings and charts show the clear relationship of *F* to the remaining MSS, but especially to T.j.l., of which *F* seems to be a continuation. An excellent article, clearly reasoned.

1919

98   Aita, Nella, "Miniature spagnole in un codice fiorentino", *Rassegna d'Arte*, XIX (1919), 149-55.
An attempt to determine which of three proposed artistic schools weighs most heavily in the production of the *CSM* miniatures: the Italian school, proposed by Amador (1863); the French, proposed by Valmar (1889); or the local schools, proposed by Durrieu (1893). No definitive conclusions are reached but the inclination is towards some more local, Iberian, schools with a touch of Italianate influence. Artwork commented is from the illuminations of *F* 88 and 74 (corresponding to *cantigas* 228 and 278 in Mettmann). Also reproduced is T.j.l. 130 so that similarities may be pointed out (remembering that *F* and T.j.l. are complementary MSS).

99   Martínez Olmedilla, Augusto, "Las desdichas del Rey Sabio", *Blanco y Negro*, no. 1480 (28 Sept., 1919), [pp. 15-17].
A brief summary of the high and low points of Alfonso's several careers as monarch, soldier, poet, historian, etc. Written as a prelude to the 700th anniversary of his birth in 1921.

100   Michaëlis de Vasconcellos, Carolina, "No seio da Virgen-Mãe", *Lusa*, II (1919), 145-6. Cited but never located. I quote from a reprint in *No seio da Virgen-Mãe: Sôbre a história de uma quadra popular* (Viana-do-Castelo: Biblioteca da Revista *Lusa*, 1922). 27 pp.
The author's is one of three brief studies of the Incarnation as expressed in the image of the sun's rays piercing a window pane and leaving it intact. The pertinent *cantiga* is 413.

1920

101   Nunes, J.J., "Uma lenda medieval: O monge e o passarinho",

Boletim da Segunda Classe, Academia das Sciencias de Lisboa (Coimbra), XII (1917-18 [1920]), 389-405.
A study of several accounts of the legend taken up in *cantiga* 103 which circulated in the Middle Ages, both before and after Alfonso's account, in Latin as well as in the vernaculars. The original comparative notes offered by N. as he searches for a probable source are of especial value.

102 Pedrell, Felipe, *Cancionero musical popular español*, III (Barcelona: Editorial Valls, 1920?), pp. 1-6 [musical examples]. 2nd ed. (Barcelona: Casa Ed. de Música Boileau, n.d.), pp. 1-2 [text], 1-6 [musical examples].
P. adds to those he published in 1918 the music and partial texts of two *loores* (*CSM* 200 and 230) and two *miragres* (*CSM* 61 and 65). A harmonized version of the last of these is called a "fifth" *cantiga*.

1921

103 Aita, Nella, "O códice florentino de *Cantigas* de Affonso, o Sábio", *Revista de Língua Portuguesa*, no. 13 (1921), 187-200; no. 14 (1921), 105-28; no. 15 (1922), 169-76; no. 16 (1922), 181-8; no. 18 (1922), 153-60. Later published as a monograph, with the same title (Rio de Janeiro: *Revista de Língua Portuguesa*, 1922). 91 pp.
A.'s long 5-part article is her thesis, Florence, 1919. It complements Solalinde's work on the same MS (1918). There are a few inconsistencies in the listing of *loores* (p. 189, n. 10, and again on p. 193), but these minor infractions are overshadowed by the very real accomplishment of A.'s case – based on a re-ordering of the Florence MS's jumbled folios – for this MS's kinship to its paleographic twin, Escurial MS T.j.l. She comes close to establishing *F* as the copy once possessed by Lucas Cortés and seen by Zúñiga (1677). The miniatures of *cantigas* 228, 292, and 278 (*F* 88, 10, and 74), the technical aspects of the illumination, and the metrical variety of *F* are taken up in the article's second part, which ends with an Italian translation of strophe 3 of *F* 86 (Mettmann's 409). Parts 3, 4, and 5 present variants for 53 *cantigas* (not noted by Valmar [1889] but incorporated into Mettmann's ed. [1959]).

104 Gili, Samuel, "Una nota para las *Cantigas*", *RFE*, VIII (1921), 60-2.
Following the work of Arco (1915) on the location of Salas in the poems of the *CSM*, G. further demonstrates how faulty was Valmar's location of this town in the region of Lérida, for there it was always accentuated Salás. Concludes that the misconception derives from *CSM* 168 in which the female protagonist is from Lérida but makes her pilgrimage to Salas in

Huesca. It is unlikely that two *santuarios* are alluded to, and with this judgment of G.'s it is easy to concur.

105   Michaëlis de Vasconcellos, Carolina, "Glossário do *Cancioneiro da Ajuda*", *Revista Lusitana*, XXIII (1920 [1921]), 1-95. Also publ. as a monograph with the same title (Lisbon: A.M. Teixeira, 1922). xii + 95 pp.
A companion to her edition of *Ajuda* (1904), it served for years as an important source for meanings of words in the other *cancioneiros* which lacked such a glossary. It is still of some use.

106   Ribera y Tarragó, Julián, "Valor de la música de las *Cantigas*", *Discursos leídos ante S.M. el Rey (23 de nov. de 1921) . . . para conmemorar el VII centenario del nacimiento del rey Don Alfonso el Sabio* (Madrid: Tip. de la *Revista de Archivos*, 1921), pp. 7-20. Rpt. in the author's *Disertaciones y opúsculos*, II (Madrid: Impta de Estanislao Maestre, 1928), pp. 3-16.
An introd. to modern versions of the music of *CSM* 1, 30, 68, 118, 124, 174, 184, 242, 322, and 391, reconstructed by the author and harmonized by Tomás Bretón Hernández. Although Arabic music is not recorded in modern notation until the sixteenth century, Ribera argues that Arabic melodies that Alfonso heard in his youth must have been the inspiration of the music of the *Cantigas*. Even more extraordinary is the further claim that Arabic music was also the source of the regional music of Aragon, Asturias, and, ultimately, of medieval music throughout Europe. See also Riaño (1887).

1922

107   Bell, Aubrey F.G., *Portuguese Literature* (Oxford: Clarendon Press, 1922), pp. 37-57.
Chapter 2, "The Cancioneiros", begins with a history of the songbooks which, excepting *Ajuda*, all contain poems by Alfonso. Bell is always interesting reading; here he deals succinctly with Alfonso's choice of Galician-Portuguese (p. 41) and the personal nature of the *CSM* (pp. 42-4), and he praises the artistry of the *loores* (p. 45). This section, though brief, is accurate. The later pages are devoted to other poets, chiefly to Alfonso's grandson, King Dinis of Portugal.

108   Ribera y Tarragó, Julián, *La música de la Cantigas. Estudio sobre su origen y naturaleza con reproducciones fotográficas del texto y transcripción moderna* (Madrid: RAE, 1922).
Although R.'s claims for Arabic genesis of both the form and the music of the *CSM* have largely been dismantled (see Anglés, 1943), the first

section of this study – dealing with old written accounts of performances of and treatises on Arabic music – is still useful and readable. However, his conclusion, on the basis of his own work on the later *Cancionero de Palacio*, that the *CSM* was a vessel which carried Arabic music forward has but the shakiest of undocumented foundations. His theory cannot be put to the proof. Furthermore, no Arabic musical notation survives from this period; thus, Ribera seems to argue from the strength of his faith alone.

R. reproduces, in black and white, the 40 miniatures of musicians from MS J.b.2. The Toledo MS is reproduced in facsimile and twelve plates from Escurial MS J.b.2. are provided for the sake of comparison. There are transcriptions of the melodies of all 128 *cantigas* from Toledo, and 24 are fully harmonized for piano (these were released as a *tirada aparte* in the same year). As comparison, there are four melodies of Marcabru. One note of caution: Ribera does not use the MS numbering and users must consult his own pp. 148-56 for the key to his numbering. See also Riaño (1887).

109   Solalinde, Antonio G., ed., *Alfonso X, el Sabio. Antología*, I (Col. Granada, Madrid: Jiménez Fraud, 1922), pp. 5-112. Rpt (Colección Austral, no. 169, Madrid: Espasa-Calpe, 1941; often reprinted).
The first anthology of consequence. The introd. carries good accounts of the legends surrounding Alfonso. S. notes, too, that the *CSM* employs differing levels of language according to changing subject matter. *CSM* anthologized are: Prol. B, 4, 9, 56, 60, 64, 94, 132, 142, 144, 180, 195, 279, 396, 401, and the *mayas* – 406. Profane poems included are: *CBN* (in the order in which they appear in the text) 437, 439, 441, 413, 414, 416, 419, and 421.

1923

110   Bertoni, Giulio, "Alfonso X di Castiglia e il provenzalismo della prima lirica portoghese", *Archivum Romanicum*, VII (1923), 171-5.
Interprets Alfonso's criticism of Pero da Ponte, *CV* 70, to mean that the best Provençal models were not imitated by da Ponte, which weakened his quality as a poet. There are, relevant to *CV* 79, 77, and 74, and to *CB* 370, 360, and 365, discussions of Alfonso's admiration for Provençal poetic models. Bertoni's view, accepted by many, began a continuing debate on this particular strophe's meaning.

111   Callcott, Frank, *The Supernatural in Early Spanish Literature, Studied in the Works of the Court of Alfonso X, el Sabio*

(N.Y.: Inst. de las Españas en los Estados Unidos, 1923). 151 pp.

Nearly all of the *CSM* are mentioned in this essentially chatty volume (C.'s Columbia Univ. Ph.D. thesis, 1923) which provides a classification scheme according to the nature of the supernatural events that take place in the various *cantigas*. Divisions are oriented through Alfonso's own definitions of *milagro, diablo, conjuro* (taken from the *Siete partidas*, the *Primera crónica general*, the *General estoria*, and other Alfonsine works as well). There is a useful index of names and, for its day, a respectable bibliography (discounting many typographical errors). The drawback is that very little is added to our knowledge in the limited space given over to discussion.

1924

112   Garnelo, P. Benito, O.S.A., "La música de las *Cantigas*", *Ciudad de Dios*, no. 136 (1924), 130-47, 204-25, and 440-57; no. 137 (1925), 204-13.

A long and eulogistic summary of Ribera (1922), attributing to him a breakthrough of vast importance. In substance, it amounts to a defense of the Arabist theory on the development of Spanish (and European) musical forms, but is, unfortunately, not a sound espousal of the theory.

113   Menéndez Pidal, Ramón, *Poesía juglaresca y juglares: aspectos de la historia literaria y cultural de España* (Publicaciones de la *RFE*, VII, Madrid: Centro de Estudios Históricos, 1924). viii + 488 pp.

Still useful are the sections on the international character of medieval minstrelsy (pp. 50-74) and the portrayal of the poetic activity at Alfonso's court (pp. 186-259), in which Alfonso is seen as both patron and practitioner of the poetic arts. *CSM* 172 and 194 and *CV* 64, 68, and 70 are cited as elements in the portrayal of this court activity. Illustrations from *CSM* 1, 76, 93, 120, 136, and 194 actually depict it. The games and poetic repartee of society, at several levels, bring to life the ambience in which Alfonso created his own enduring monument.

114   Menéndez y Pelayo, Marcelino, *Obras completas: Varia*, III (Madrid: CSIC, 1958), pp. 219-40.

MMP gave lectures to the Ateneo, Madrid, at the turn of the century, dealing with *CSM*, Valmar's edition (1889), and the attributed poems. Full texts have not survived, but newspaper summaries are here reprinted, with Julio Puyol y Alonso's account of one lecture, which he published in 1924.

115   Sardinha, António, "A música das *Cantigas*", *Lusitania*, I

(1924), 91-106.

A mostly approving review-article on Ribera (1922) with enough reservations about the theories expounded there to make it worth consulting. Disagrees strongly, and rightly, with one particular contention – that the *CSM* represent nascent poetic forms.

116 Sunyol, P.D. Gregori Maria, "Cantigues de Montserrat del rei Anfós X, dit 'el savi' ", *Analecta Montserratensia*, V (1922 [1924]), 361-417.

S. gives the six Montserrat *cantigas* detailed exposition and analysis. For each of them – *CSM* 48, 52, 57, 113, 302, and 311 – he provides a transcription based on Valmar's (but not slavishly so), a facsimile of the text and the musical notation from MS J.b.2., and, since S. found Ribera's 1922 system of transcribing the music into modern notation inadmissible, his own version of the music for these Alfonsine contributions to the so-called "Cantoral de Montserrat". The texts are not totally accurate (see Bohigas, 1925).

117 Villecourt, Louis, "Les Collections des Miracles (arabes) de la Sainte Vierge", *Analecta Bollandiana*, XLII (1924), 21-68, 266-87.

Though these miracles date from the seventeenth century the accompanying notes contain a wealth of condensed information on analogues in various languages (e.g., Latin, French, Ethiopian, Arabic) of miracles appearing in the *CSM*. For example, no. 1 of the Arabic series is *cantiga* 2 (San Ildefonso) and there are listed ten other locations of this narration, complete with MS number.

1925

118 Bohigas, Pedro, [untitled review in] *RFE,* XII (1925), 304-5.
Reviews Sunyol's art. of 1924 and lists the misreadings found in the versions given of the six Montserrat *cantigas.*

119 Crane, Thomas Frederick, ed., *Liber de miraculis sanctae Dei genetricis Mariae* (Ithaca, N.Y.: Cornell Univ. Press, 1925). This is the collection of Bernard Pez, printed originally at Vienna in 1731. The notes to its miracles indicate other locations of the narrations. These include the *CSM* and a summary chart is printed on pp. 118-19. Easy to use.

120 De Lollis, Cesare, "Dalle *cantigas de amor* a quelle *de amigo",* in *Homenaje ofrecido a Ménendez Pidal* (Madrid: Ed. Hernando, 1925), I, pp. 617-26. Rpt. in *Cervantes reazionario e altri scritti d'ispanistica* (Firenze: G.C. Sansoni, 1947), pp. 229-49.

Late in this study, De L's discussion of the title theme leads again to those poems of Alfonso critical of Pero da Ponte, notably *CV* 70. De L. suggests that the criticisms might not imply that Pero da Ponte was too "popular", i.e. not a "classical" troubadour like Bernaldo de Bonaval, but rather that he borrowed too freely from Eannes de Cotom (a point of information also supplied by Alfonso in his poem, *CV* 68). De L. thus disagrees with Michaëlis de Vasconcellos (1904), vol. II, pp. 456 ff.

121   Filgueira Valverde, J., "Cantigas d'El-Rey Sabio localizadas en Galicia, San Ero de Armenteira", *Nós* (Orense), no. 21 (1925), 4-5.
Gathered here are important data for the study of the sources and the historical background of the miracle of the monk who fell enraptured for centuries listening to the melodious song of a bird (Alfonso's version is found in *CSM* 103). In Galician. (See also Filgueira Valverde, 1926.)

121 bis (1925) See p. 115.

122   López Aydillo, Eugenio, "El siglo XIII en los cancioneros gallego-portugueses", *Homenaje ofrecido a Menéndez Pidal* (Madrid: Ed. Hernando, 1925), II, pp. 619-31.
A general article which sketches the poetic trends of the thirteenth century in NW Spain, and has implications for the grafting of foreign — mostly Franco-Provençal — poetic modes onto a flourishing popular lyric, the suitability of certain poetic genres and styles to the *cancioneiros*, and the standards of composition employed and admired in that era. The author sees society genuinely reflected in these poetic songbooks and treats them as both sociological and historical documents. Not very convincing, as he does not account for the presence of poetic conventions, which do not always share the daily reality of human life.

123   Peláez, Mario, "La leggenda della Madonna delle Neve e la *CSM* 309 di Alfonso el Sabio", *Homenaje ofrecido a Menéndez Pidal* (Madrid: Ed. Hernando, 1925), I, pp. 215-23.
A contribution to the future accounting of the sources of the *CSM*. The article recounts the known Italian legends, poems, and artworks that celebrate the miraculous ninth-century event at Rome. Alfonso's *cantiga* 309 is thought to be a personal reworking of a confused version (the tale is not included in miracle collections generally circulated), which somehow retains the main points while sacrificing some of the more poetic evocations of the likely original.

1926

124   Dexter, Elise F., "Sources of the *Cantigas* of Alfonso el Sabio",

unpubl. diss., Univ. of Wisconsin, Madison, 1926.
Eighty-eight of the *CSM* which have international sources (as cited by Valmar) are studied. The format of each mini-study includes: 1) a synopsis; 2) a bibliography; 3) a discussion; and 4) a separate conclusion. The second section of each comes mostly from Mussafia (see introduction) and the Ward-Herbert *Catalogue of Romances in the British Museum*. The *cantigas* studied are: 2, 4, 6-9, 11-17, 19, 21, 23-9, 32-9, 41-2, 45-7, 49, 51, 53-4, 56, 58, 61-3, 65-8, 71-6, 79, 81, 84-9, 94, 101, 105-6, 115, 125, 128, 131-2, 139, 154, 175, 195, 206, 216, 231, 254-5, 265, 269, 281, 285, 298, 308, 362, 384, and 402 ("Saturday").
Conclusions offered are that Alfonso was characteristically free in following his source, especially with regard to names, speech, and homely details, and that Adgar, Berceo, and the French MSS were little used while Vicent of Beauvais, Gautier de Coincy, Hugo Farsitus and the miracles collected by Bernard Pez in 1731 were more closely followed both in factual material and in narrative order. Much useful material is summarized in these small studies. However, after nearly fifty years, much expansion is needed.

125   Filgueira Valverde, José, "A lénda d'Armenteira (notas de folk-lore)", *Nós* (Orense), no. 25 (1926), pp. 10-12; no. 26 (1926), pp. 9-11.
An outline of sleeper legends in the Middle Ages and later. The spells are cast by sight, sound, smells, etc. Analogues to *cantiga* 103 are found in Portugal, Navarre, Picardy, France, Belgium, Sweden, Wales, Ireland, Germany, and Austria. Others come from early non-Christian sources. These two parts of a series of articles (see also Filgueira Valverde, 1925) paraphrase the contents or events of most of these analogues. The notes tell where most can be located.

126   Magne, Augusto J., "Afonso X, o Sábio. *CSM*. Excerptos annotados", *Revista de Língua Portuguesa*, VIII, no. 44 (1926), 55-110.
These *cantigas* were to form part of a longer, unrealized, book of texts plus glossary. They follow Valmar with a few insignificant adaptations and include: Prol. B, 1, 10, 20, 30, 50, 60, 320, 70, 80, 140, 200, 210, 250, 260, 290, 300, 340, 350, 401, 402, and 406. The most useful parts are the brief notes and variants which accompany the texts.

127   Trend, J.B., *Alfonso the Sage and Other Spanish Essays* (London: Constable and Co., Ltd., 1926), pp. 11-17.
Trend's attitude is that the *CSM* are mostly "jingles and music", that "dancing dactyls" are preeminent among the metrical feet, and that sound dominates sense. He is too harsh overall but does refer to an

artistic unity for the *CSM*, a hint few scholars have taken up.

128 —, *The Music of Spanish History to 1600* (Oxford: The Univ. Press, 1926), pp. 52-65, 201-8.
Leans heavily on Aubry (1906 and 1908) and expands very little on the essay listed above. Ready acceptance of an Arabic imprint on the poetic forms but not on the music of the *CSM*. On pp. 201-8 T. prints some musical versions, after Aubry, but they are better consulted, by the musicologist, in the original place.

1927

129 Anglés, Higinio (amb la versió catalana pel Dr. Josep Mª Llovera), *Les "Cantigas" del rei N'Anfós el Savi* (Barcelona: Impr. d'E. Subirana, 1927). 64 pp. An offprint from vol. XIV of *Vida Cristiana*, 1927.
Seven shorter studies which accomplish several things: 1) establish that no musicologist should take seriously the work of Ribera (1922) on the *CSM* (see esp. pp. 42 and 54-7); 2) print musical transcriptions which are based on sounder precepts of musicology; and 3) give metrical paraphrases, which are attempts to prevent heretical interpretations from attaching themselves to the *cantigas* selected. The latter procedure is not a happy one, even though, for most of the selections, Valmar's text is also provided. The *cantigas* taken up – in order of presentation, but with Mettmann's numbering – are: *CSM* 50 (p. 8), 424 (p. 11), 417 (p. 17), 422 (p. 20), 426 (p. 25), 427 (p. 28), 1 (p. 35), 418 (p. 38), 419 (p. 44), 411 (p. 49), 425 (p. 58), 413 (p. 60), and 100 (p. 63). Pertinent musical remarks are made *passim*.

130 Arraiza, Francisco Javier, "Sobre la historia de las *Cantigas*. Un libro de Julián Ribera", *Boletín de la Comisión de Monumentos Históricos y Artísticos de Navarra*, 3rd series, I (1927), 263-74.
A serviceable if somewhat adulatory presentation of Ribera's 1922 vol. on the music of the *CSM*. This is but the first of a projected series of articles which rehash the entire book and it will have little value except, perhaps, to a scholar interested in the reactions to Ribera's interesting theories. No further instalments were published (at least in this journal). A. mistakenly lists Eslava's musical transcription as of *CSM* 15: it is actually number 14 (see Eslava [1865] and Rioja [1866]).

131 Guiette, Robert, *La Légende de la Sacristine. Étude de littérature comparée* (Paris: Librairie Honoré Champion, 1927). 554 pp.

The subject is treated in great detail and with vast erudition by G. The theme of the Virgin Mary substituting for errant nuns goes from the earliest Latin accounts recorded through 1927. Cotarelo y Valledor's study of 1904 is dwarfed in comparison. *CSM* 94 and 55 are dealt with (pp. 111-15), the first as a fused and the second as a contaminated version but both unique in the thirteenth century, and, Guiette claims, with genuine élan and artistry. *CSM* 285, on a related theme, is given briefer mention (p. 175).

132   Rey, Agapito, "Índice de nombres propios y de asuntos importantes de las *CSM*", *BRAE*, XIV (1927), 327-55.
A useful supplementary index to the Valmar ed. Catalogues names of people and places in the *CSM* and provides some brief notes and references. It needs now to be revised and expanded, but it can still be used as a mostly reliable guide.

133   Ribera y Tarragó, Julián, *Historia de la música árabe medieval y su influencia en la española* (Madrid: Voluntad, 1927). 355 pp.
Synthesis of two earlier volumes, *La música de las Cantigas*, 1922, and *La música andaluza medieval en las canciones de trovadores, troveros y minnesinger*, 1923-5. Defends again the fundamental belief that if a poetic idea is adopted, its form and music may be as well. Only the final two chapters deal directly with the *CSM* and these ideas. The very tenuous nature of this treatment is always obvious.

1928

134   Mazzei, P., "Del *Tesoro* di Alfonso X e dei processi alchimistici", *Archivum Romanicum*, XII (1928), 139-49.
Another voice in the modern chorus justifying the rejection of the verse *Tesoro* as part of the Alfonsine poetic canon. M. shows, on the basis of the contents, that it can only have been drafted after 1400, thus confirming Moratín's judgment (1830).

135   Rey, Agapito, "Correspondence of the Spanish Miracles of the Virgin", *Romanic Review*, XIX (1928), 151-3.
A supplement to the listing in Crane (1925). Rey adds to the lists, for comparison of contents, the collection by Alfonso's contemporary Gil de Zamora, the *Liber Mariae*. There are errors, unfortunately. *CSM* 54, not 34, corresponds to *LM* 19, and Berceo's *Milagro* 23 should be not where it is placed but in the same column as *CSM* 25 and *LM* 13. One error is corrected by Rey: Crane listed *CSM* 37 as the equivalent of Berceo's *Milagro* 13 but this should be *cantiga* 87.

1929

136 Domínguez Bordona, Jesús, *Exposición de códices miniados españoles: Catálogo* (Madrid: Sociedad Española de Amigos del Arte, 1929), pp. 74-89.
Alfonsine miniature style is treated although rather superficially. Still, the main characteristics of the MSS are given in handy summary form.

137 Poch Noguer, José, *Alfonso X, el Sabio. Relato de su vida sin paralelo* (Barcelona: Ed. Araluce, 1929, 2nd ed., 1942, 3rd ed., 1956). 144 pp.+ 9 plates.
Reader beware! This is a poeticized and patriotic account, designed for adolescents, which includes dialogues. Credits Alfonso with introducing the lyric element into Castilian (p. 83). To be avoided as biography or as fiction.

138 Ribera y Tarragó, Julián, *Music in Ancient Arabia and Spain,* trans. and abridged by Eleanor Hague and Marion Leffingwell (Palo Alto, Calif.: Stanford Univ. Press, 1929, rpt. N.Y.: Da Capo Music Reprint Series, 1970). 283 pp.
Ribera approved this translation and abridgement of his opus of 1922. The condensation omits points that were intended for the Spaniard or the Gregorian specialist. The result is not very edifying. The section treating the *CSM* appears between pages 177 and 255.

139 Rodrigues Lapa, Manuel, *Das origens da poesia lírica em Portugal na Idade Média,* I (Lisbon: Seara Nova, 1929).
L. often asserts that the *CSM* are erudite and not popular compositions, but the supporting arguments for this contention are not spelled out in this volume. Later, Lapa will modify these ideas: his study of the *CSM* over many years has shown that some measure of popular inspiration is present.

1930

140 Domínguez Bordona, Jesús, *La miniatura española,* II (Florence: Pantheon, 1930), pp. 38-42, plus 9 unnumbered sepia tint plates.
The MS miniaturists are accorded high praise for the integration into the *CSM* of the broad canvas of contemporary Spanish society and are perceived to have been trained in the French manner, although with a few Italian traits. These artists were, unfortunately, anonymous. The coverage here is solid despite the lack of room for detail. The plates are not of good quality (there are representatives from all three of the MSS that have miniatures: J.b.2 and T.j.l, both of the Escurial, and the

one housed at the Biblioteca Nazionale in Florence).

141   Gil Salguero, Luis, ed., *Las Cantigas de Santa Maria* (Montevideo, 1930).
This work is cited by G. London (1960) but my searches have not been able to locate it.

142   Margelí, Antonio, "Las *Cantigas* de Alfonso X el Sabio. Su notación en colores", *Ritmo* (Madrid) (August 30, Sept. 15, October 15 and 30, 1930). Rpt. in *Revista Eclesiástica*, III (1931), 176-97.
I cite from the latter (first instalment of *Ritmo* version not seen). This is for specialists in medieval mensuralist notation. M. attempts to establish that the color (red or black, but sometimes black and white) of notes is an important key to interpretation of medieval music. All arguments here are tentative as the system changes from place to place with the schools of notation. They are further undermined by the lack of any direct precedent for Alfonsine notation. The motive behind the publication of this unusual item is the desire to identify the *jota* melodies with certain of the *CSM*. The whole idea is just too difficult to accept and is dismissed by Anglés (1943) as fanciful.

143   Spanke, Hans, "Die Theorie Riberas über zusammenhänge zwischen frühromanischen Strophenformen und andalusisch-arabischer Lyrik des Mittelalters", *Volkstum und Kultur der Romanen*, III (1930), 258-78.
This analysis of Ribera's basic works (1912, 1922) lauds their enthusiasms and pinpoints their scholarly failings. These include the weak and sometimes non-existent documentation and the lack of real musicological expertise. The positive thrust of this study, however, is to show that Alfonso can be placed squarely on the line of development of western music which is, in part at least, liturgical. This latter position has been documented by Anglés whom S. has read closely and well. This is sound and convincing argumentation for the prosecution.

1931

144   Anglés, Higinio, *El Còdex musical de Las Huelgas: Música a veus dels segles XIII-XIV*, I (Barcelona: Institut d'Estudis Catalans, Biblioteca de Catalunya, 1931), pp. 51-8.
These few pages cover much ground. They establish a probable polyphonic musical basis in the courts of Fernando III and Alfonso, both of whom were musicians. They renew disagreements with Ribera (1922) about European music's being rooted in Arabic music and suggest persuasively, with musical examples from Ripoll, that the

predominant musical forms of the *CSM*, the *rondeau* (*cantiga* 279) and the *virelai* (*cantigas* 52 and 425), were preceded by non-Arabic western originals.

145ʹ Fernández Núñez, Manuel F., *Las canciones populares y la tonalidad medieval* (El Escorial: Real Monasterio de El Escorial, [1931]). 108 pp.
A clear and sometimes bitter exposition of how often Ribera's 1922 volume on the *CSM* and its link to Arabic music is incorrect. Almost all of R.'s statements are held up to the light of critical analysis and found wanting. Perhaps the grossest error, according to this author, is Ribera's rejection of ditonality in the *CSM* in favour of a non-existent chromatic scheme. Musicologists might take pleasure in this item but it is hard on others.

1932

146 Donostia, José Antonio de, *Tres cantigas de Alphonse X/Trois cantilènes d'Alphonse X*, version française de Henri Collet, musique de Antonio-José (Paris: Max Eschig, 1932). 11 pp.
These *cantigas* of Alfonso (*CSM* 139, 221, and 28) have been prepared for voice and piano.

147 Nunes, José Joaquim, *Cantigas d'amor dos trovadores galego-portugueses* (Coimbra: Univ., 1932, rpt. N.Y.: Kraus Reprint Co., 1971. New ed., Lisbon: Centro do Livro Brasileiro, 1972).
Here is a critical edition of three Alfonsine compositions, *CB* 360-2 (Nunes' nos are XXV-XXVII). Brief comments on Alfonso are to be found on pp. xxx-xxxi.

148 Sánchez Pérez, José Augusto, *"Libro del tesoro*, falsamente atribuido a Alfonso el Sabio: una nueva copia encontrada en la Biblioteca de Palacio de Madrid", *RFE*, XIX (1932), 158-80.
A look at a newly-uncovered MS of the poetic *Tesoro*, at one stage often attributed to Alfonso X. The introd. to the edited text gives explicit information on the false attributions.

149 Zarco Cuevas, P. Fr. Julián, *Catálogo de los mss catalanes, valencianos, gallegos y portugueses de la Biblioteca de El Escorial* (Madrid: Tip. de Archivos, 1932). 164 pp.
Minute descriptions of MSS J.b.2 and T.j.1 (pp. 107-14). These are essentially those that appeared in Valmar (1889), which were prepared by Paz y Melia. Zarco Cuevas has added bits of information. Plates of

cantigas 165 and 62 from T.j.1 and of 145 and 10 from J.b.2 and a short bibliography are additional features.

1933

150 Rodrigues Lapa, Manuel, ed., *Textos de literatura portuguesa, I: Afonso X, o Sábio* (Lisbon: Imprensa Nacional, 1933). viii + 103 pp.
This anthology of 34 *cantigas* was the result of the author's desire to make the *CSM* more accessible. Edition based on J.b.2, as was Valmar's (1889). A major difference seems to be Lapa's lack of hesitation in representing true palatals with the modern graphs -nh- and -lh- and in the use of accentuation to aid the reader. *Cantigas* appearing here are: 1, 2, 5, 8-10, 16, 20, 24, 36, 56, 70, 84, 94, 103, 128, 155-6, 200, 206, 211, 250, 260, 316, 322, 335, 351, 353, 369, 372-3, 340, 401, plus the *mayas* (Mettmann no. 406). An adequate glossary is included.

151 Rübecamp, R., "A linguagem das *CSM* de Afonso X o Sábio", *Boletim de Filologia*, I (1933), 273-356; II (1934), 141-52.
A trans. of part of R.'s doctoral diss. (Hamburg, 1930), this article deals with Romance hiatus in the *CSM*, the Galician-Portuguese *cancioneiros*, and older Galician docs in an attempt to determine what, if any, significant distinctions might turn up in comparisons between them. Using Valmar and, for the Florence MS, Solalinde (1918), R. shows that the poetic language of the *CSM* and of the *cancioneiros* lags behind the spoken language (represented by certain aspects of the docs), thus confirming the statements of Michaëlis de Vasconcellos in *ZRP*, XXVIII (1904), p. 217. For the matter of hiatus in particular, the *CSM* show traces of divergence from the *cancioneiros*, a division which is true as well for their general phonetic and morphological features. Were it not for conservative trends in literary styles, R. feels that the *CSM* would more clearly show the development of Galician away from its Portuguese counterpart, a trend wholly supported by the less conservative docs from the same period. Interesting reading.

152 Sánchez Pérez, José Augusto, "Una bibliografía alfonsina", *Anales de la Universidad de Madrid – Letras*, II (1933), 188-214, 289-311.
The first large-scale attempt to gather the growing mass of critical literature on Alfonso and his works. Contains over 600 entries, even with omissions (and some erroneously placed material). Especially valuable for editions, MSS, and the like. Approximately 40 entries deal with Alfonsine poetry (under "Alfonso" and the sub-heading "Cantigas"). None of these is annotated. There is no index.

1934

153   Garrido Merino, Edgardo, *La saeta en el cielo: Leyendas místicas de la Edad Media* (Madrid: Espasa-Calpe, 1934). 178 pp.
Alfonso is compared to Solomon in a light introduction which is followed by the author's imaginative recreation, in prose, of ten of the *CSM*. Inspired by the text and the miniatures, these tales bear little relationship to their prototypes. Compare *cantiga* 154, for example, to the title legend.

154   Marullo, Teresa, "Osservazioni sulle *Cantigas* di Alfonso X e sui *Miracles* di Gautier de Coincy", *Archivum Romanicum*, XVIII (1934), 495-540.
Direct textual comparison of the *CSM* and MS Pal. Lat. 1969 of Gautier's *Miracles de Nostre-Dame* which convincingly demonstrates that in both content and formal expression Alfonso knew his French predecessor's work better than Valmar first thought (1889). Other sources available to Alfonso are also considered by M. but none comes close, numerically speaking, to Gautier's work. Fullest comments are given to *cantigas* 6, 8, 15, 28, 51, 54, 65, 33, and 56. Less space is given over to *cantigas* 4, 5, 7, 11, 13-14, 16-17, 24-6, 32, 34-7, 42, 45-7, 53, 58, 61, 66-8, 71, 81, 105, 115, 132, 255, 285 and 362.

155   Pope, Isabel, "Mediaeval Latin Background of the Thirteenth-Century Galician Lyric", *Speculum*, IX (1934), 3-25.
Obviously a very general article. However, the student of rhythm and prosody in the *CSM* will want to be aware of the many parallels from Latin literature presented by Pope.

156   Rodrigues Lapa, Manuel, *Lições de literatura portuguesa: Época medieval* (Lisbon: Centro de Estudos Filológicos, 1934, 345 pp.; 7th ed., Coimbra: Coimbra Editora, 1970, 441 pp.).
R. L. added to this work over the years but its thrust is basically unchanged. The entire first half (Parts 1-5) is pertinent to the general poetic background of Alfonso's age: aspects of troubadour culture, genres and metres, origins, language, etc. Particularly valuable with regard to the *CSM* are the evaluations of the theories of lyric origins, the final section of Part 3 (on the Rocamadour-based *miragres*), and Part 4, section 3, which takes up the subject of the poetic attacks on Maria Balteira and stresses the importance of the many-faceted *cantiga d'escarnho* (citing *CV* 74, 77, and 79 of Alfonso) for the dating of poetry. R.L. knows most of the studies previous to his and synthesizes

them expertly, making his discussions, though brief, usefully comprehensive.

157 Wyrembek, Anna, and Jósef Morawski, *Les Légendes du "Fiancé de la Vierge" dans la littérature médiévale. Essai de synthèse* (Poznańskie Towarzystwo Przyjaciol Nauk Prace Komisji Filologicznej, Tom VII, Zeszyt 3, Poznan, 1934). 60pp.
Although none of the *CSM* is discussed directly, this work contains much that is important to a full study of the sources and analogues of *cantiga* 42, esp. those in Latin and in French.

1935

158 Anglés, Higinio, *La musica a Catalunya a fins al segle XIII* (Barcelona: Institut d'Estudis Catalans, 1935). xvi + 447 pp.
There are references *passim* to the *CSM*, some quite interesting. Shows the *virelai* forms present in Latin verse prior to Alfonso (p. 256). Confirms Spanke's opinion that *CSM* 279 is a modified *rondeau* (p. 343). Theorizes about the *CSM*'s influence on the Catalan troubadour Cerverí (p. 343). Discusses how it may be shown – with *CSM* 12 as an example – that mixed modal rhythm was already developed in the Peninsula (pp. 352-3). Notes similarities to the *CSM* in a song by Arnaut de Marueill, *ca* 1170-1200 (p. 394).

159 Ballesteros y Beretta, Antonio, *El itinerario de Alfonso el Sabio. I: 1251-59* (Madrid: Tip. de Archivos, 1935). 232 pp.
Useful for the further documentation of Alfonso's devotion to Mary through his especial generosity to Marian churches and shrines, particularly those of the Benedictine and Cistercian Orders.

159 Hisan, Pedro (pseud.), "Los orígenes del culto de Santa María
bis del Puerto, 1255-1500", *Guión* (Jerez de la Frontera), no. 16, pp. 3-4; no. 17, pp. 19-20; no. 18, pp. 1-2, no. 19, pp. 1-2; no. 20, pp. 4-5 (all 1935).
This article in five parts, despite the dates in its title, covers only the period of Alfonso's reign. The first part explicates *CSM* 328 as showing Alfonso's predilection for Puerto de Santa María, since documents show that this *cantiga* has much historical accuracy. The second part takes up the Military Order of Santa María de España which Alfonso founded and which had one of its four bases in Puerto de Santa María (see also Pérez Villamil [1806], and Menéndez Pidal [1907]). Alfonso's special patronage of the city is developed in part three, through the texts of *CSM* 358, 364, and 367. The latter poem is fully explicated in

part four, which also implies that Alfonso was sole author of the *CSM*. The last part lists 22 *CSM* written by Alfonso as the "juglar" of Puerto de Santa María: 328, 356-9, 364, 366-8, 371-2, 375-9, 381-2, 385, 391, 393, and 398 (he omits two others, 389 and 392). See also item 363, below.

160 Nolasco, Flérida, "Las *Cantigas* de Alfonso el Sabio: Origen y antigüedad de los ritmos antillanos", *Orto* (Manzanillo, Cuba), XXIV (1935), 109-15 [Cited by G. London (1960), p. 26, but never located.]. Rpt. in the author's *De música española y otros temas* (Santiago de Chile: Ediciones Ercilla, 1939), pp. 11-22.
N. maintains that the rhythms of Caribbean creole music (and even of some Viennese waltzes) have come to us from Greece through Andalusia and, specifically, through such collections as the *CSM*. Even troubadours and minnesänger only had to invent new lyrics for these Andalusian melodies (p. 18). This item is uncritical, fanciful and unsupported by anything other than N.'s reading of Ribera (1922). Even then, his ideas are here stretched to the limit of credibility.

161 Pellegrini, Silvio, "Sancio I o Alfonso X?", *Studi Romanzi*, XXVI (1935), 71-89. Rpt. in the author's *Studi su trove e trovatori della prima lirica ispano-portoghese*, 2nd ed. (Biblioteca di Filologia Romanza, III, Bari: Adriatica Editrice, 1959), pp. 78-93.
Subject is *CB* (MS) 456. Michaëlis de Vasconcellos (1904) had convinced most scholars that Sancho I of Portugal, founder of Guarda (mentioned in the text of the poem), himself wrote the poem. P. argues that "guarda" is not necessarily a place name, and presents valid reasons why it ought not be considered so. He restores *CB* (MS) 456 and the following poems through 466 to the pen of Alfonso X. This attribution is now taken for granted.

162 Sánchez Pérez, José Augusto, *Alfonso X el Sabio, siglo XIII* (Madrid: Aguilar, n.d. [1935]). 301 pp.
Sections included are "Vida", "Obras", "Ideario", "Bibliografía", and an anthology. The whole is very general but, given that, it serves as a reliable introduction to Alfonso's career. The bibliography is the same as the listing of 1933 with the addition of some 115 items of which few are on Alfonso's poetry. The anthology prints: *CSM* Prol. B, 10, 107, and 256; *CV* 73 and 74; and *CB* (MS) 468, 472, and 474-6. There are no notes. No index.

163 Sancho de Sopranís, Hipólito, "Los orígenes del culto a Santa María del Puerto, 1255-1500", *Guión* (Jerez de la Frontera), nos. 16-20 (1935), no pages cited.

Listed thus by Martínez Alfonso (1962) and S. de S. (1964), but clearly a reference to 159 bis, which S. de S. published under the pseudonym Pedro Hisan.

1936

164 Filgueira Valverde, José, *La Cantiga CIII: Noción del tiempo y gozo eterno en la narrativa medieval* (Santiago de Compostela: Univ., 1936). 219 pp. + 8 plates.
The author's doctoral diss. Part I discusses visions and voyages, miraculous sleeper and survivor legends as a preface to an understanding of the thematic inheritance of *cantiga* 103. Part II deals with transmission of the legends, their geographical spread, and their appeal in Cistercian circles. Alfonso's was the first version to incorporate the tale of the monk enraptured by birdsong for 200 years into the Marian framework (pp. 90-6). Part III takes up themes: time (both real and imagined); the power of music; the symbolic use of bird and forest, and so on. The notes and indices are fine and the depth of the study is exemplary. Few such studies on a single *cantiga* exist, especially in this comparative way. Copies are few, and it deserves reprinting.

165 García de la Fuente, P. Arturo, "Las *CSM* del Rey Sabio. Avance de un estudio artístico-descriptivo de las ilustraciones miniadas de sus códices", *Ciudad de Dios*, CLII (1936), 45-68, 371-84.
The third part of this advance notice of a longer study never appeared, owing to the Civil War; nor did the longer study. The author attempted to bring together the previous work of Salas (1877), Durrieu (1893), Amador (1874), Aita (1919, 1921) and Domínguez Bordona (1930) and expand on it. The miniatures of both the Escurial MSS are described in detail (measurements, colors, arrangement, etc.) but the author never saw the Florence MS. There are hints in this outline, however, of interesting themes lightly sketched for us: depiction of civil and military customs and peoples, the supernatural events recorded in the miniatures, the life of clerics, and the arts, especially music, of Alfonso's era. The sections to have been treated in the third part were: daily customs, private and public diversions, and Nature. For a completed discussion of these topics in Alfonsine miniatures, see Guerrero Lovillo (1949).

166 Spanke, Hans, *Beziehungen zwischen romanischer und mittellateinischer Lyrik* (Abhandlung der Gesellschaft der Wissenschaften zu Göttingen Phil.-Hist. Klasse, 3rd series, XVIII, Berlin: Weidmannsche Buchhandlung, 1936; rpt. Nedeln, Lichtenstein: Kraus, 1972), pp. 125-34.

We are reminded that not only are many of Alfonso's *CSM* direct descendants of the western *rondeau* form but previously the form had appeared in two poems by Pero da Ponte. The characteristic internal refrain is also seen in many other *cancioneiro* selections with one of several variations, indicating that Alfonso may himself have had quite an ample supply of models on which to fashion his own *rondeau*-like compositions.

1937

167   Valbuena Prat, Ángel, *Historia de la literatura española*, I (Barcelona: G. Gili, 1937, pp. 116-26; 6th ed., 1960, pp. 124-35).

V. accepts too readily the theories of Ribera but this is otherwise a fairly good and compact general introduction to Alfonso's poetry. It concentrates on a wide classification of the narrative poems, based on that already done by Valmar in 1889. His recognition of the lyrical nature of much of Alfonsine narrative verse deserves wider acceptance and further scholarly study.

1938

168   Anglés, Higinio, "Die geistliche Musik in Spanien des Mittelalters", in *Görres-Gesellschaft zur Pflege der Wissenschaft im katholischen Deutschland. Jahresbericht* (Bonn, 1938), pp. 59-76.

Only the final pages touch on the *CSM*, whose MSS A. has been studying for his future edition (1943). In addition to taking the opportunity to again disparage Ribera's 1922 study of the music of the *CSM*, the author discusses the rhythmic nuances and the dramatic representation of the mystico-religious element in the *CSM* as a whole which makes the Alfonsine compilation, in terms of medieval music, unique.

1939

169   ——, "La música de las *Cantigas de Santa María* del Rey Don Alfonso el Sabio", *Radio Nacional: Revista Semanal de Radio-Difusión* (1939-40), 14-15.

This is one of twelve brief articles (all with the same title, apparently) appearing over the course of the year in *Radio Nacional.* In barely six columns of text, A. manages, persuasively, to support his contention that Alfonso was an accomplished musician and that Fernando III, his father, was also. Alfonso's contemporaries knew this and there was, consequently, much polyphonic interchange between Spain and France, where Alfonso's cousin, Louis, was on the throne. Alfonso endowed a chair of music at Salamanca, one more indication of his interest in music. A. argues – with the musical transcriptions of *CSM* 361 and 347 – that the texts themselves tend to provide proof of Alfonso's intervention as composer of the pieces.

170 ——, "La notación mensural de la música monódica de la corte española del siglo XIII ofrece soluciones nuevas, hasta hoy totalmente desconocidas, para la interpretación estético-rítmica de las melodías de los trovadores", a discourse delivered by proxy to the American Musicological Society of New York (Sept., 1939).
The text, so far as I know, has not been preserved but the information is incorporated into Anglés's full study of this question (1958). The illustrations for the lecture were preserved and printed (Barcelona: A. Boileau y Bernasconi, 1939. 4 pp.). These include the J.b.2 notation of the incipits of *CSM* 179, 28, 10, 57, 2, 159, 292, 24, 303, 209, 353, and 47. It was through A.'s study of musical notation of the Alfonsine MSS that his decoding of the songs of the troubadours and the trouvères was made possible.

1940

171 ——, "Hispanic Musical Culture from the 6th-14th Century", *Musical Quarterly*, XXVI (1940), 494-528.
Adapted from the author's *Còdex musical* (1931). The *CSM* are portrayed on pp. 524-8. The familiar arguments are presented: particular combinations of text and music are present in Latin works of 1200 and earlier and the musical patterns are close to those of the French *virelai*. Examples repeated from the earlier work are *CSM* 425 and 52.

172 Lusarreta, Pilar de, "La amada de Alfonso el Sabio", *La Nación* (Buenos Aires) (31 de marzo, 1940), 2nd section, no pagination.
An account of Alfonso's love for Doña Mayor de Guillén and the birth of their daughter Brites (Beatriz), with gruesome accounts of later depositions concerning e.g. Doña Mayor's coffin. The only connection with Alfonso's poetry seems to be the belief that Mayor's beauty inspired the emotion of the refrain of *CSM* 10. Quite to the contrary, it is the Doña Mayor type that Alfonso explicitly rejects in *cantiga* 10. Article of no real value to anyone.

173 Reese, Gustave, "Spanish Monody: the *Cantigas*", in *Music in the Middle Ages* (N.Y.: W.W. Norton, 1940), pp. 244-8.

Brief discussion of the *CSM* highlighted by rejection of Ribera's theory of Arabic origin of the melodies of Alfonso's songs. Reese takes the opposite view, i.e. that Christian usage (the *virelai* and related strophic forms) may have influenced the *zéjel*. Anglés's early transcriptions of the music merit high praise from Reese; there is less enthusiasm for Aubry (1906, 1908) and his follower, Trend (1926). A brief bibliography appears on pp. 450-1.

174   Sánchez Cantón, Francisco J., "Seis estampas de la vida segoviana del siglo XIII", *Correo Erudito*, I (1940), 332-4.
Harkens back to Fita's article on the subject (1886) and delves into characteristics of the illuminations from MS T.j.l (Escurial) of *cantiga* 107. Noted are a propensity to caricature and some irregularity of detail. Despite this, however, there still remains a fairly faithful image of medieval Segovia.

1941

175   Carter, Henry Hare, ed., *Cancioneiro da Ajuda: A Diplomatic Edition* (Modern Language Association of America, General Series, XIV, N.Y.: Modern Language Association, 1941). xvii + 190 pp.
The introd. shows why the previous edition (Michaëlis de Vasconcellos, 1904) has led to some incorrect linguistic conclusions. There are abundant plates and three indices: 1) cancellations; 2) marginal notations; and 3) lacunae.

176   Chase, Gilbert, *The Music of Spain* (N.Y., 1941, and London: J.M. Dent & Sons, 1942; 2nd ed. N.Y.: Dover, 1959) pp. 26-30, 34-5, and 230.
Brief and general account of the musical nature, origins (following Anglés), and MS depictions of the *CSM*. Only one musical example is supplied – *cantiga* 425, on p. 28. Four miniatures of musicians are reproduced on a plate between pp. 32 and 33.

177   Filgueira Valverde, José, *Da épica na Galicia medieval*, Discurso de ingreso na Real Academia Gallega, 1941 (Vigo: Artes Gráficas Galicia, 1973). 26 pp.
A small portion of the address (published 32 years after delivery) is relevant to the *CSM* but it is provocative: the 74 consonant lines (no refrain) of *cantiga* 420 are akin to the epic laisse. Other *cantigas* with reminiscences of epic song are 5, 369 (in *cuaderna vía*), 95, 63, 181, and 205 (not 155, as is printed), especially in their conformity to metrical requirements.

178 Sánchez Castañer y Mena, Francisco, "La pecadora penitente en el teatro español: Sus fuentes y evolución", unpubl. thesis, Univ. of Madrid, 1941.

Nuns are protagonists in *CSM* 7, 55, 94, 285, 58, and 59. Secular women are featured in *cantigas* 17, 104, 151, 399, 98, 272, 305, 213, 237, 115, 201, 64, 312, 26, and 68. Related cases are recounted in nos 5, 107, 185, 125, and 195.

1942

179 Asín Palacios, Miguel, "El juicio del P. Mariana sobre Alfonso el Sabio", *Al-Andalus*, VII (1942), 479.

A note for those interested in following this Alfonsine legend. A.P. draws a parallel between an old Arabic anecdote about an astrologer of Alexander the Great's court and the unflattering blasphemy attributed to Alfonso: "Dumque coelum considerat observatque astra, terram amisit".

180 Pellegrini, Silvio, "Noterelle alfonsine (Su *A* 256)", *Studi Romanzi*, XXIX (1942), 131-7. Rpt. in the author's *Studi su trove e trovatori della prima lirica ispano-portoghese*, 2nd ed. (Biblioteca di Filologia Romanza, III, Bari: Adriatica Editrice, 1959), pp. 117-21.

In *Ajuda* 256 Payo Gomes Chariño compares the sea to a king, possibly Alfonso. P. believes the unnamed sovereign referred to is indeed Alfonso, and his argumentation in defense of this position is clever. Curiously, P. notes, the same image also appears in Alfonso's own *Siete partidas* II.ix.28.

181 Salazar, Adolfo, "Poesía y música en las primeras formas de versificación rimada en lengua vulgar y sus antecedentes en lengua latina en la Edad Media", *Revista de Filosofía y Letras* (Mexico), IV (1942), 287-349. Rpt. in the author's *La música en Cervantes y otros ensayos* (Madrid: Ínsula, 1961), pp. 59-126.

Not very useful. The *CSM* are listed as containing many zejelesque forms with *virelai* musical patterns (p. 73) and *cantiga* 10, with the same form, has *ballade* music (p. 103). Two of the secular lyrics, *CBN* 419 and 421, seem on the surface to be variants of *rondeau* forms.

182 Torres Balbás, Leopoldo, "La mezquita de Al-Qanātir y el santuario de Alfonso el Sabio en el Puerto de Santa María", *Al-Andalus*, VII (1942), 417-37.

Recounts architectural history using both historical and poetic accounts, some from the *CSM*. It permits the accurate dating of some of these miracles for the years 1260-72. There is a surprising amount of poetic evidence which complements — or at least does not contravene — the notarial docs the author presents.

183 Wilkes, Josué, ["Cantiga 10"] in *Joya de canciones españolas*, prologue and selection by E.M. Barreda (Buenos Aires: Asoc. Patriótica Española, 1942), pp. 7-9.
Wilkes harmonized *cantiga* 10 and the Castilian version was supplied by Barreda. His harmonization is, in part, due to his grave disagreements with the transcriptions of Ribera (1922).

184 —— , "La XI cantiga de Alfonso el Sabio, y su armonización por Julián Ribera", Offprint from *Revista del Profesorado* (Buenos Aires, 1942). 16 pp.
For musicologists only. This is a highly technical discussion of Ribera's harmonizations (1922) and especially of that of *cantiga* 11. There is also ample discussion of the earlier work of Collet and Villalba (1911) on *CSM* 10.

1943

185 Anglés, Higinio, *La música de las "CSM" del Rey Alfonso el Sabio: Facsímil, transcripción y estudio crítico*, II (Barcelona: Diputación Provincial de Barcelona, Biblioteca Central, 1943). 126 pp. of text + 462 pp. of transcriptions.
Other vols followed in 1958 and 1964 (see entries for those years). The five opening chapters set forth, in minute detail and with scrupulous bibliographical procedure, the work done on the music of the *CSM* up to the author's time. Chap. 1 is a diary-like account of the evolution of A.'s own involvement in this not inconsiderable task. The discussion of musical notation systems is particularly valuable because it is approached historically and comparatively. Also included are an index of first lines, and a thematic index of the melodies. This volume and its later companions irreversibly established the foundation of all future study of the music of the *CSM* and even of that of the troubadours and trouvères.

186 —— , *La música en la España de Fernando el Santo y de Alfonso el Sabio*, Discurso leído el 28 de junio, 1943, ante la Real Academia de Bellas Artes de San Fernando (Madrid: Real Academia de Bellas Artes de San Fernando, 1943). 69 pp.
Pages 26-31 describe the musical court of Alfonso and speak of its richness. A. feels that the depictions of Arabic musicians do nothing to show that they were composers as well as instrumentalists. Students

of music will benefit from an illuminating discussion (pp. 36-50) of the notation and rhythms of the *CSM*. Alfonso as musician is also seriously discussed (pp. 50-3), and the musical sources of the poems are mentioned (p. 53). The reverberations of his own studies on Alfonsine music that have affected modern musicology close this condensation of many years of work by Anglés on the *CSM*.

187 Cerulli, E., *Il libro etiopico dei miracoli di Maria e le sue fonti nelle letterature del Medio Evo latino* (Studi Orientali, I, Rome: G. Bardi, 1943).
Contains analogues of *CSM* 9 (ch. 19), 2 (ch. 22-3), 115 (ch. 24), 26 (ch. 28), and 57 (ch. 41, para. 215).

188 Montes, Eugenio, *Federico II de Sicilia y Alfonso X de Castilla*, Anejo to *Rev. de Estudios Políticos*, X (Madrid, 1943). 31 pp.
Although mostly the political personalities are dealt with here, the spiritual side of Alfonso shows up in his great attachment to the Virgin Mary (pp. 14-15). One poem, *CBN* 416, is cited in discussions concerning Alfonso's difficulties in finding people in whom to place his trust.

189 Ríos Sarmiento, José, *La vida y los libros de Alfonso el Sabio* (Barcelona: Ed. Juventud, 1943). 189 pp.
Pages 161-7 are devoted to Alfonso's poetry; only the *CSM* are mentioned. This is a stringing together of quotations from other scholars and has no depth or originality, although it is generally sound.

190 Sánchez Castañer y Mena, Francisco, "Antecedentes celestinescos en las *CSM*", *Mediterráneo: Guión de Literatura*, I, no. 2 (1943), 33-90.
A satisfying and near-exhaustive study of the earliest Romance outlines of the character made famous by Fernando de Rojas. The two *CSM* which have celestinesque types are 64 and 312, especially well-delineated in the latter; treated not as sources of Rojas's creation but as earlier manifestations of a generic type. Since written sources seem lacking, much is made of local, folkloric realism in the creation of Alfonso's protagonists.

191 Sánchez Pérez, José Augusto, *El culto mariano en España* (Madrid: CSIC, 1943). 482 pp.
These are legends, tales, and accounts associated with the Marian sanctuaries throughout the Peninsula, several of which figure in the *CSM*. They are alphabetically arranged, followed by an onomastic index and several plates.

191 Sancho Mayi [Sopranís], Hipólito, *Historia del Puerto de*
bis *Santa María* (Publicaciones de la Exma Diputación de Cádiz,

Cádiz: Ed. Escelicer, 1943), pp. 3-42.

Most of the work of Hisan (1935) has been deftly absorbed into this account of the early years of Puerto de Santa María. With 24 compositions dealing with this city in the *CSM*, Alfonso's favour is clearly shown: no other city appears as often. Adduced in the commentary are *CSM* 328, 383, 371, 398, 364, 358 and 367. Pages 20-2 review the city's connection with the Military Order of Santa María de España founded by Alfonso. The author is careful to separate history from aesthetic elaboration and this enhances the value of his contribution.

192   Urrestarazu, Sinesio, "Las *Cantigas* de Alfonso X el Sabio: una modificación a la historia de la música", *Revista de las Indias*, 2nd series, XVII, no. 53 (mayo, 1943), 221-60.

A silly and overlong exposition of Ribera's theories (1922) which, paradoxically, was published in the same year as Anglés's more serious musicological studies demolishing Ribera. A notable, perhaps startling, claim is that the *CSM* were inspired by popular Castilian refrains (p. 232).

1944

193   Anglés, Higinio, "La música de las *Cantigas* del Rey Alfonso el Sabio", *Arbor*, I (1944), 327-48.

For the layman, A. presents compact information on the notation of medieval European music and the *CSM*. Discussed are the exceptional musical techniques practised at Alfonso's court, the musical variety within the range of the *CSM*, and the import of such matters for modern musicological study. This version of the first part of the text of his monumental *La música de las "CSM"* (1943) tells how his study grew from idea to reality.

194   Clarke, Dorothy Clotelle, "The Early *Seguidilla*", *HR*, XII (1944), 211-22.

C. notes how difficult it is, even from the definitions of the earliest commentators, to know exactly how the *seguidilla* as we now know it came to take recognizable shape. She suggests that a proto-form may have derived from popular song and may have included assonant and consonant rhyme both. She ventures the suggestion that the refrains of *CSM* 91, 93-5, 98, 110, 117-18, 137, 141-2, 211, 259, 298, and 370 show the *seguidilla* form, as does the entire composition of *cantiga* 134.

195   Filgucira Valverde, José, *La obra histórica y literaria de Alfonso X* (Murcia, 1944).

Cited thus in G. London's bibliography (1960), this item has not been located.

196 Sánchez Pérez, José Augusto, *Alfonso X, el Sabio,* 2nd ed., expanded and corrected (Madrid: Aguilar, 1944). 477 pp.
Almost identical to the 1935 first edition. Adds a section on the Alfonsine legends, a few extra dates and additional comments on his life. The anthology is slightly expanded (*CV* 77 is added) and a mere four items are added to the bibliography. No notes.

1945

197 Alfonso X, *Setenario,* ed. by Kenneth H. Vanderford (Buenos Aires: Instituto de Filología, 1945). lxxx + 271 pp.
Alfonso's introd. to this work contains ten sections of high praise for his father, Fernando III. These involve many segments which could be profitably used to demonstrate some literary inclinations on the part of the father which took root and flowered fully in the son.

198 Fernandes Lopes, Francisco, "A música das *CSM* e o problema da sua decifração", *Brotéria,* XL (1945), 49-70.
Reviews musical studies of Aubry (1906-8), Collet and Villalba (1911), Ribera (1922), and one early study by Anglés (1927), and rejects them all on the basis that they begin from aprioristic notions. The author claims to be seeking a way of transcribing the *CSM* that would permit words and music to combine in an intimate and natural manner: he prints his own versions for *cantigas* 10, 255, 77, and 260, in which he claims to have respected better than his predecessors the MS notation. His ideals are noble but he runs into the same pitfalls. Words and music in the *CSM,* when they do not fit each other smoothly, cannot be made to do so. Had he had Anglés's 1943 transcription, he might have revised some of this article.

199 García Moreno, María Teresa, "¿Cuáles son los orígenes musicales de las *Cantigas*?", *Boletín de la Real Academia de Ciencias, Bellas Letras y Nobles Artes de Córdoba,* XVI (1945), 67-70.
This is a summary of GM's induction address, the original being lost. It seems to have been a careful review of the facts about music in Spain that exposed Ribera's (and others') exaggerations about the Arabic influence on the *CSM.* At the induction, eight *cantigas* (258, 406, 327, 306, 179, 354, 126, and 4) were sung to piano accompaniment. I have not been able to discover whose arrangements these were.

200 Guerrero Lovillo, José, "Muebles hispanoárabes en las *Cantigas* de Alfonso el Sabio", *Al-Andalus,* X (1945), 432-40.
Only pp. 437-40 deal with Alfonso's works. Three *cantigas* are cited for their illustrations, with sketches by the author: 169, 110, and 165.

These all contain examples of Arabic furniture, mostly thrones and royal seats. They correspond to plates 185, 122, and 180 in his major work published in 1949, *q.v.*

201   Pellegrini, Silvio, "Alfonso X (rapido profilo)", *Glauco*, I (1945), 9-10. Rpt. in the author's *Studi su trove e trovatori della prima lirica ispano-portoghese*, 2nd ed. (Biblioteca di Filologia Romanza, III, Bari: Adriatica Editrice, 1959), pp. 122-8.
Alfonso seen as an unlucky king but a capstone of medieval civilization. Poetry seen as a prime activity and Alfonso's relations with Guiraut Riquier, his poetic jests involving Maria Balteira, Pero da Ponte and others, his calculated ingenuousness (a good observation), and the technical virtuosity of both his profane and religious output. These are all points deftly and swiftly made, but without detail.

202   Procter, Evelyn S., "The Scientific Works of the Court of Alfonso X of Castille: The King and His Collaborators", *MLR*, XL (1945), 12-29.
Valuable and thoroughly documented short history of the roles of Alfonso and his international collaborators in the scientific works that bear the royal rubric. Not of direct interest for the poetry, but must be taken into account when reading the articles by Solalinde (1915) and G. Menéndez Pidal (1951) on the way Alfonsine works came about.

1946

203   Cardenal de Iracheta, Manuel, ed., *Alfonso el Sabio, selección y notas* (Biblioteca Literaria del Estudiante, 29, Madrid: CSIC, 1946). 246 pp., esp. 229-37.
Contains only *cantiga* 4, taken from Valmar.

204   Krappe, Alexander H., "Our Lady of Rocamadour and the Two Gamblers", *HR*, XIV (1946), 164-7.
Although not a perfect match with any of the known tales, *CSM* 214 has interesting parallels with parts of five of them. These are quoted by K.

205   Schneider, Marius, "A propósito del influjo árabe: Ensayo de etnografía musical de la España medieval", *Anuario Musical*, I (1946), 31-141.
By bringing to bear over one hundred musical examples on the question of Arabic influence on Spanish music, S. shows that any such claims are truly tenuous. There are, however, some common features of the two owing to eastern origins of both. Ribera (1922) is shown not to have

the musicological background for such an ambitious project as he attempted and to have provided false (and even atypically Arabic) transcriptions of the *CSM*. Bibliography and maps are included in this very acute study.

206   Spanke, Hans, "La teoría árabe sobre el origen de la lírica románica a la luz de las últimas investigaciones", *Anuario Musical*, I (1946), 5-18.

Densely written and persuasively reasoned argument against the Arabic-origins theories, principally those of Ribera (1912, 1922). The Latin *conductus* and the vernacular lyric are similar in both metrical and strophic form, and some are even similar melodically. S. favors a sociological approach to the debate; he posits the adaptation of closer European (e.g., Latin) models for the birth of the Romance lyric. His study shows the *zéjel* to have little in common with the *virelai*, especially as in the *CSM*. The Arabists' theories strain belief, first and foremost because they are unnecessary, and then because they are insufficiently supported by evidence.

207   Thomas, Sir Henry, *Monstruo y milagro: El gallo resuscitado* (Oxford: The Univ. Press, 1946). 20 pp.

Note 5 calls to attention that this tale has an analogue in Alfonso's *cantiga* 175, with a different and somewhat less dramatic ending in the latter. (This note is absent from the 1935 version of this pamphlet, in English.)

1947

208   Costa Pimpão, Álvaro J. da, *História da literatura portuguesa*, I: *Idade Média* (Coimbra: Atlântida, 1947; 2nd ed., 1959), pp. 71-2, 133-45.

Pages 71-2 (ed. of 1959) advance the notion that Alfonso takes Pero da Ponte to task in *CV* 70 for not singing the praises of Mary. This is a new and appealing view in a continuing debate on the meaning of this poem's critical assessment of da Ponte. A longer section, pp. 133-45, contains a general summary which is also noteworthy for some original thinking about such Alfonsine matters as Maria Balteira, the use of Galician-Portuguese for the *CSM*, and the possibility of an earlier flowering of religious lyric in that idiom. The author praises *cantiga* 330 as one of the finest of all the early lyric songs.

209   Entwistle, William J., "Dos cossantes às cantigas de amor", in *Da poesia medieval portuguesa*, ed. by A.F.G. Bell, 2nd ed. (Lisbon: Ed. Revista *Ocidente*, 1947), pp. 75-99, esp. 94-6.

E. observes that the *CSM* are not akin, by type or structures, to Alfonso's secular poetry. He praises the parallelistic usage encountered in *cantigas* 250 and 260 and remarks on the breadth of Alfonso's contact with indigenous, popular poetry of which kind the *mayas, cantiga* 406, is given as an example.

210   Fernandes Lopes, Francisco, "A 183ª das *CSM*" (Faro, 1947). Cited in Filgueira Valverde (1949), p. 639, but not yet located.

211   Llampayas, José, *Alfonso X, el hombre, el rey y el sabio* (Madrid: Biblioteca Nueva, 1947). 255 pp.
A book to be avoided. Conceived as a poetic kind of history, it is semi-novelized and told in the present tense. Pages 64-8, for example, recreate a musical evening at Alfonso's court featuring the performance of the king's own *cantiga* 256. Alfonso is later seen dying in the arms of his daughter, Queen Beatriz of Portugal, who sings *cantiga* 10. Needless to say, there is no documentation for anything.

212   Parra, Benito García de la, *Versión coral de sesenta CSM del Rey Alfonso el Sabio: Precedida de un breve estudio de los antiguos modos, como base de su realización armónica* (Madrid: Sociedad Didáctico Musical, 1947). 157 pp.
Presented for choral singing are: *CSM* 1-15, 18-25, 27-9, 33, 35, 39-42, 44-5, 48, 51-2, 54, 56-60, 64, 67-8, 76-8, 83, 86, 93, 96, 113, 117, 123, 126-7, 136, and 302. The transcriptions are based on those of Anglés (1943). The purpose is to make these songs more widely accessible for performance. Useful notes on notions of musical modes in liturgical song as well as some others on problems of harmony are contained in the prologue written by Conrado del Campo.

1948

213   Anglés, Higinio, *Gloriosa contribución de España a la historia de la música universal*, Discurso pronunciado en la sesión de clausura del VII pleno del Instituto Español de Musicología (Madrid: CSIC, 1948). 62 pp.
Pages 30-2 have capsule remarks on the diversity of the music of the *CSM*; while there are *lacunae* in the range of religious melodies (esp. when contrasted with that available for courtly music), the *CSM* have helped fill some of these *lacunae*.

214   Castro, Américo, *España en su historia: cristianos, moros y judíos* (Buenos Aires: Losada, 1948), pp. 340-6. The same study is also found in the author's *La realidad histórica de España* (Mexico City: Porrúa, 1954), pp. 351-6, as well as in the revised English version of the 1948 book, *The Structure of*

Spanish History, trans. Edmund L. King (Princeton; Univ. Press, 1954), pp. 361-8.

C. projects, inconclusively, the idea that the *zéjel* form, predominant throughout the *CSM*, betrays more than contact with Arabic poetry; it reveals a community of values that touch the innermost regions of artistic life. To illustrate this, he brings in *cantigas* 169, 4, 6, 54, and 56. C. is almost always interesting; however, these remarks illuminate his own more general theories and manage to shed little light on the *CSM* as a work all its own.

215   Fernandes Lopes, Franciso, "Uma *CSM* no cancioneiro de Colocci-Brancuti", *Brotéria*, XLVI (1948), 733-9.
Treats of *CSM* 40 (also 467 in Colocci-Brancuti; *CBN* 409) which the author claims is inaccurately transcribed by Anglés (1943). Parallel transcriptions are offered of the Toledo MS (now at the BN) and Escurial J.b.2 and the author supplies his own modern interpretation of the music. Not enough solid argumentation is included for a conclusion to be drawn on the issue.

1949

216   Baraut, Cebrià, "Les *Cantigues* d'Alfons el Savi i el primitiu *Liber Miraculorum* de Nostra Dona de Montserrat", *Estudis Romànics*, II (1949-50), 79-92.
Treats the possibilities of both written and oral development of the six *CSM* which record events in which the Black Virgin of Montserrat is featured: 48, 52, 57, 113, 302, and 311. It is 48 and also 302 which may have utilized written sources, similar to those that Baraut discusses here. There is a misprint on p. 80: *CSM* 437 should read 347.

217   Bernadou, Pierre, *Alphonse le Savant* (Geneva: Éditions Suzerenne, 1949). 255 pp.
Overall a weak presentation. Alfonso as poet is the subject of ch. 6 (pp. 135-65) and as a musician, of ch. 7 (pp. 166-84). B. follows Valmar in making Alfonso a reader of Berceo as well as in most of the details of biography. The treatment of music is a disaster since less than a page is given over to the real point under discussion. The poetic texts are cited in French trans., to no useful end.

218   Filgueira Valverde, José, "Lírica medieval gallega y portuguesa", in *Historia general de las literaturas hispánicas*, I, ed. G. Díaz-Plaja (Barcelona: Barna, 1949), pp. 543-642.
A competent study of the entire period and the poetry and polemics accompanying it. Emphasis is on the secular *cancioneiros*, but the *CSM* are also treated (pp. 599-604). Best of all, the "orientación

bibliográfica" which is, in part, annotated, is erudite, felicitously arranged by topics and remains useful for initial study of most all aspects of the poets and personalities that enliven the Galician-Portuguese lyric.

219   Frank, István, "Les Troubadours et le Portugal", in *Mélanges d'études portugaises offerts à M. Georges Le Gentil* (Lisbon: Inst. para a Alta Cultura, 1949), pp. 199-226.

A summary of all the most reliable information about poetic activity before, during, and after the time of Alfonso X. Of background utility only as no specific texts are discussed.

220   Guerrero Lovillo, José, *Las Cantigas: Estudio arqueológico de sus miniaturas* (Madrid: CSIC, 1949). 435 pp. + 212 black and white plates.

A monumental study. The working text is a richly detailed examination of clothing – secular and ecclesiastical, male and female attire, the dress of Moor and Jew – and of architectural and artistic forms. These cover civilian and military structures, lay and religious edifices, painting and sculpture, inscriptions, glassware, ceramics and other interior and exterior decoration, all enhanced by the author's sketches. For the plates, MS T.j.1 was used. A door is opened onto the world of the thirteenth century. A solid introd. and good indices give further breadth to this study. For some further comments, see Sánchez Cantón, 1949.

221   Le Gentil, Pierre, *La Poésie lyrique espagnole et portugaise à la fin du Moyen Âge*, 2 vols (Rennes: Plihon, 1949, 1952). Vol. I, pp. 297-311; vol. II, pp. 319-62, 410-54 *passim.*

Vol. I treats the *CSM* as a genre called the pious lyric in which Alfonso is credited with being creative and original in the use of models; for example, his use of the *virelai* often exceeds the allowable length for the French original and the *tornada* is nearly always discarded. More erudite forms, without refrain, can be seen in other sub-genres: the Joys of *cantiga* 1 and the Sorrows of *cantiga* 403.

Vol. II demonstrates that most all of the standard poetic forms of the fifteenth century are present in the *CSM*. Alfonso's *marial* is especially important for transmission of the *virelai* form, both as a structure and as a musical piece in which a melodic line for use in the refrain is borrowed from the strophe. Le G. is always respectful of Anglés's study of the music (1943) and A.'s transcriptions allow him to review Clarke's suggestions (1944) about the *seguidilla* and further suggest that only *CSM* 91, 93, 94 and 98 – refrain only for the four – and 134 in its entirety are probable forerunners of that form (II, p. 442, n. 10).

222 Machado, Elza Pacheco, and José Pedro Machado, eds, *Cancioneiro da Biblioteca Nacional, antigo Colocci-Brancuti: Leitura, comentários e glossário*, 8 vols (Lisbon: *Revista de Portugal*, 1949-64).
The full *CB* published for the first time, as only a portion was edited by Molteni (1880). The ed. is not truly critical, but it lists variants, contains notes and, very important, has facsimiles of the MS. The onomastic list and the glossary in vol. VIII are very good. Alfonso's *CBN* poems carry the numbers 398-441, 1424, and 1528. Many of the readings given are tentative. More reliable are the texts as given by Rodrigues Lapa (1965, 2nd ed. 1970).

223 Sánchez Cantón, Francisco J., "La vida en España en los tiempos del Rey Sabio", *Arbor*, XIV (1949), 471-8.
Essentially a review-article on Guerrero Lovillo (see 1949, above). The most helpful part of the article points out the many things about the "vida multiforme de aquella España": travel, architecture, music, agriculture, daily occupations, pastimes, games, and so forth. The point is made that no MS reveals as fully as T.j.l. what that world looked like and we need be thankful Alfonso was so desirous of having the *CSM* illuminated.

1950

224 Kline, Lawton Brain, "A Metrical Study of the *CSM* by Alfonso el Sabio", unpubl. diss., Stanford University, 1950.
The problems studied here, with great profit, include: Castilian influence at work in utilization of favoured narrative meters, esp. the octosyllable; predominance of Provençal traits in the *loores* (as distinct from the narrative *cantigas*; the influence of the *zéjel* on the rhyme scheme of the *CSM*; and problems the music creates for the form and construction of the texts when a melody exists first and the lyrics must be made to conform.

225 Martins, Mário, "A Assunção de Nossa Senhora, na poesia medieval", *Brotéria*, LI (1950), 531-9.
Examples are given, from all the principal European poetic traditions of the Middle Ages, of the Assumption of the Virgin. They include *CSM* 419 (pp. 534-6) for which parts of the text are used in paraphrase. There is no poetic analysis.

226 Saraiva, António José, *Historia da cultura em Portugal*, I (Lisbon: Jornal do Fôro, 1950), pp. 128-39, 297-314.
This introduction to popular and palace poetry makes very worthwhile reading. Alfonso's court, poetic practices, and influence are integrated

into a nicely etched overview of the thirteenth and fourteenth centuries. See S.'s index for specific page nos.

227   Torres Balbás, Leopoldo, "Miniaturas españolas medievales", *Al-Andalus*, XV (1950), 191-202.
Another review-article on Guerrero Lovillo (1949). However, extends the concept of a rev. to show further, through comparison with Hispano-Arabic miniatures from other MSS, that the *CSM* illuminations are rooted in French styles and share nothing with the truly oriental schools of manuscript art. The author concludes that the *CSM* miniatures represent a purely Hispanic art.

1951

228   Brittain, Frederick, *The Medieval Latin and Romance Lyric to A.D. 1300*, 2nd ed. (Cambridge: Univ. Press, 1951). 274 pp.
A 60-page study and an anthology of Latin, Provençal, French, Castilian, Galician-Portuguese and Italian lyrics. Alfonso is represented by *CSM* 10 and *CBN* 414, his sole surviving Castilian poem (a fragment). The supporting apparatus (indices, bibliography, list of sources for texts) is good overall but, obviously, not extensive for Alfonso X.

229   Fernández del Riego, Francisco, *Manual de historia de la literatura gallega* (Vigo: Editorial Galaxia, 1951; 2nd ed. 1971; 3rd ed. 1975).
The first edition is in Castilian, subsequent ones in Galician. The biographical sketch on Alfonso is too brief to be of major value (pp. 37-9, 1st ed.; pp. 47-9, 3rd ed.), but the entire vol. gives some definition to what Alfonso's poetic court must have been like. The Academy ed. (1889) of the *CSM* is still referred to even in 1975, over a full decade after the entire series of Mettmann vols (the best edition) was readily available. One black and white plate (facing p. 33, 3rd ed.) is provided.

230   Martins, Mário, "Milagres e romarias portuguesas, nas *CSM*", in *Peregrinações e Livros de Milagres na nossa Idade Média* (Lisbon: Edições Brotéria, 1951; 2nd ed., 1957), pp. 71-87.
No textual analysis is offered; rather, an attempt is made to use the relevant *CSM* to form a picture of the activities associated with the visitation of shrines and the making of pilgrimages. The results are a kind of rhymed chronicle utilizing *cantigas* 322 (for which a rendering into modern Portuguese is given), 238, 327, 342, 237, 399, 245 (and not CCXV as printed), 222, 369, 338, 277, 316, and 318. However, more dramatic force is obtained from the integrated view presented by the group of Santa Maria de Terena miracles: *CSM* 197-9, 223-4, 228, 275, 283, 319, 333, and 334. Most of these accounts reached Alfonso

by word of mouth although at Évora (reported in *cantiga* 338) there seems to have been a book of the Virgin's miracles which is now unknown or else lost forever.

231   Menéndez Pidal, Gonzalo, "Cómo trabajaron las escuelas alfonsíes", *NRFH*, V (1951), 363-80.
The most thorough survey of the topic since Solalinde's (1915). The author establishes, through texts of translations and compilations, the periods of greatest activity and the organization of Alfonso's writing teams. A complete list of names of collaborators, based on all existing reports and docs, is furnished. The general remarks on the *CSM* seem tentative but the illuminations of Alfonso, captured in the characteristic attitude of dictating to his scribal teams, are believed to have documental force (given the corroborating textual evidence).

232   Neuvonen, Eero K., "Los arabismos de las *CSM*", *Boletim de Filologia*, XII (1951), 291-352.
Each of the 47 *arabismos* is studied and analysed in context and also in comparison with original meanings in Arabic. Some are learned; others seem to have entered through Castilian. A few seem independent of either solution. These make up approximately 1 per cent of the 235,286 words in the *CSM* in contrast to the thirteenth-century average for the Peninsula of about 4 per cent. One of the paradoxes brought out by this study is that direct contacts between the Arabic world and the Galician-Portuguese, although frequent, did not produce much observable direct linguistic borrowing, Galician resorting to Castilian as an intermediary for such borrowings.

233   Procter, Evelyn S., *Alfonso X of Castile: Patron of Literature and Learning* (Oxford: Clarendon Press, 1951). vii + 149 pp.
These are the Norman Maccoll Lectures, originally delivered in 1949. We get the historian's viewpoint on two important phases of Alfonsine poetic activity in Ch. 3, on the *CSM*, and in Ch. 6, on the king and his collaborators. The former chapter features a summary of major scholarly work on the *CSM* to date, a discussion of its lyric nature and content, and the notion that this work belongs primarily to the literary history of Portugal. The mentions of personal involvement on many levels carries over to Ch. 6 in which *cantigas* 209, 169, 360, 180, 279, and 401 are adduced for support of the author's views on Alfonso's intimate participation in the successive editions of the *CSM*. This is an intelligent, cautious, and sensitive appraisal.

234   Ruiz y Ruiz, Lina A., "Gonzalo de Berceo y Alfonso X el Sabio: los *Milagros de Nuestra Señora* y las *Cantigas*", *Universidad de San Carlos*, XXIV (1951), 22-90.

Long but padded with brief biographical sketches, plot summaries, etc. The author, who uses the Ebro ed. of Berceo and Solalinde's anthology of Alfonso (1922, 1941), has no real room to work in as so few of the *CSM* are in Solalinde. She is able to match up only three of the *Milagros* to the *CSM* but makes very little of her opportunities. On the whole, too elementary and too incomplete.

235   Varela Jácome, Benito, *Historia de la literatura gallega* (Santiago de Compostela: Porto, 1951), pp. 28-33.
General and not always accurate. Galician locales are singled out for discussion (*CSM* 22, 26, 77, 104, 187, 304, 352). One useful feature is a listing of local variants of the Beatriz legend (*cantiga* 94), its forms and popularity.

1952

236   Alegría, José Augusto, "As *CSM* de Afonso X, o Sábio", *Revista de Portugal*, XVII (1952), 285-96.
The text of an address on aspects of the *CSM* which was accompanied by the performance of six in concert. The choicest remarks deal with the history of musical study of the *CSM* in the last two centuries, in which the Arabist theory comes off poorly. Readers should note that on p. 293 the name Menéndez Pidal is an error for Menéndez Pelayo, and that Alfonso became king in 1252, not 1232 (p. 294).

237   Álvarez Blázquez, José María, ed., *Escolma de poesia gallega*, I: *1198-1346* (Vigo: Galaxia, 1952), pp. 127-37.
A brief biography of Alfonso, in Galician, and texts of *CSM* 10, 103, 260, 351, and 406, plus *CV* 63, 73, and 79.

238   Anglés, Higinio, *Las Cantigas del Rey Alfonso el Sabio, fiel reflejo de la música cortesana y popular de la España del siglo XIII* (Murcia: Academia Alfonso X el Sabio, 1952). 18 pp.
The text of what must have been a public address by the most erudite musical scholar working in this field. There is a satisfactory sketch of Alfonsine musical culture, even though limited by its modest intentions. Focusses on the popular dance melody and Gregorian chant while making a case for the entirely monodic nature of the music of the *CSM*, despite the earlier introduction of polyphony. Ends by cautiously suggesting that some internal evidence might help lay a foundation for demonstrating Alfonso's actual participation as a composer of some *cantiga* melodies.

239   Fernandes Lopes, Francisco, "Uma cantiga de Santa Maria", *Las Ciencias*, XVII (1952), 119-28.

CSM 15 and Anglés's musical transcription of it come under attack. Anglés used, as a base for his work, Escurial J.b.2, while F.L. is convinced that the Toledo codex of the *CSM* (now at the BN) offers a better means of capturing the correct rhythmic notation of the *cantiga*. In order to show how his own system is preferable to Anglés's he prints the latter's transcription next to his own and provides photographs of the actual medieval notations from the MSS. Musicologists will decide this, but two things weaken F.L.'s claims to superiority: his system is not really spelled out for us; and we never learn what is his critical basis for telling what is musically authentic in terms of medieval sounds.

1953

240   Baraut, Cebrià, "Nota a la *Cantiga* LVII d'Alfons el Savi", *Estudis Romànics*, IV (1953-4), 205-9.
Suggests that *cantiga* 57, ascribed to the miraculous intervention of the Virgin of Montserrat, is derived from a local fusion of two separate miracles which are unmistakably connected with Rocamadour in France. B's reasoning is persuasive.

241   Pellegrini, Silvio, "Due poesie d'Alfonso X", *Studi Mediolatini e Volgari*, I (1953), 167-86. Rpt. in the author's *Studi su trove e trovatori della prima lirica ispano-portoghese*, 2nd ed. (Biblioteca di Filologia Romanza, III, Bari: Adriatica Editrice, 1959), pp. 94-116.
The two poems are *CB* (MS) 489 and 490, both of which deal with the same "meestre Johan". P. deduces, fairly, that this person is to be identified with João Alfonso of Compostela, archbishop there from 1238 to either 1264 or 1267. Satisfactory versions of both texts are printed from photographs (with variants) and there is a line-by-line annotation replete with information, etymologies, resolution of ambiguities in word meanings, plus a bonus of interpretations and paraphrases. A very laudable study of these two poems. The method is highly praised in *Filologia Romanza*, II (1955), 98-9, by G. Sansone.

242   Salazar, Adolfo, *La música de España* (Buenos Aires: Espasa-Calpe, 1953), pp. 90-112. Also 2 vols (Col. Austral, 1514-15, Madrid: Espasa-Calpe, 1953), see esp. I, pp. 113-32.
S.'s information concerning the varied background of the monodic music of the *CSM* derives unchanged from Valmar (1889) and Anglés (1943) and his attempt to use less technical terminology leads to oversimplification of the issues. The best points are those in which he describes the use of mixed musical modes and in which he compares the instruments depicted in Escurial MS J.b.2 with those mentioned in the

Libro de buen amor (Ducamin's ed., st. 1227-34 and 1513-17) and in the *Libro de Alexandre* (st. 1383, Willis ed.). Plates V-VIII complement the text with some nice illustrations of musical instruments and players.

243   Subirá, José, *Historia de la música española e hispanoamericana* (Barcelona: Salvat, 1953), pp. 117-52, esp. 123-34.
Little that is new since S. is closely adhering to Anglés (1943). There is, on p. 130, an account of how P. Burriel helped spread the erroneous view that the Toledo MS was the earliest extant. The miniatures of musicians in Escurial MS J.b.2 are reproduced and a list of the names of the various instruments is on pp. 131-2.

244   Varela Jácome, Benito, *Poetas gallegos. Las mejores poesías* (Santiago de Compostela: Porto, 1953), pp. 30-9.
Alfonso is represented by *CV* 79, *CB* 348, and *CSM* 406, 10, and 154. Texts are not at all critical.

1954

245   Castro y Calvo, José María, *La Virgen y la poesía* (Barcelona: Univ., 1954).
Fifty pages of general introduction to the topic in Spanish letters followed by a European anthology from many centuries. Only *CSM* 1 is here but the introd. may prove helpful as a guide to the Marian phenomenon in Spain.

246   Keller, John E., "A Note on King Alfonso's Use of Popular Themes in his *Cantigas*", *Kentucky Foreign Language Quarterly*, I (1954), 26-31.
For the non-specialist mainly. Brief resumés are given for *CSM* 141, 107, 258, 241, 18 and 128, all with folkloric content. One assumption, on p. 27, that the audience for Alfonso's Galician songs was unquestionably erudite, needs modification. There is also the suggestion that the comprehension of Galician-Portuguese in Alfonso's Castile was not very extensive beyond "men of letters", and this opinion clearly needs further documentation before it can be adopted.

247   —— ,"Old Spanish *Garpios*", *HR*, XXII (1954), 228-31.
CSM 212 provides the model for the use of the verb *garpir*, previously misunderstood in what had been thought of as its unique appearance in Old Spanish, in the *Libro de los engaños*. It appears in the *CSM* six times and once more as a noun, so was obviously more widespread in Galician-Portuguese than in Castilian. To these, Mettmann later adds two additional occurrences of the verb in the *CSM* (in vol. IV of his edition [see 1959]).

248 Le Gentil, Pierre, *Le Virelai et le villancico: Le problème des origines arabes* (Institut Français au Portugal, Collection Portugaise, IX, Paris: Société d'Éditions "Les Belles Lettres", 1954). 279 pp.
Important evaluative review of the major critical approaches to the origins of Romance verse forms in general and of the *virelai,* so prominent in the *CSM,* in particular. Le G. favours the idea of independent genesis, i.e. not dependent on Arabic models, and then a development consonant with liturgical advances. Appendix IV contrasts metrical and melodic patterns in the *CSM* in support of Le G.'s opinions on this matter. There is an up-to-date bibliography.

249 Rübecamp, Rudolf, "Satzphonetische Erscheinungen aus den *CSM* von Alfons dem Weisen", in *Homenaje a Fritz Krüger*, II (Mendoza, Argentina: Univ. Nacional de Cuyo, 1954), pp. 283-303.
A detailed analysis of the varied effects of hiatus on rhyme, rhythm, and metre. Concludes that hiatus plays a very important role in the *CSM* even though variations inhibit accurate prediction of its performance.

250 Westrup, Jessie A., "Medieval Song", in *Early Medieval Music up to 1300* (Vol. II of *The New Oxford History of Music*, ed. by Dom Anselm Hughes, London: Oxford Univ. Press, 1954), pp. 220-69.
In a chapter on song which seems solid despite the need to compress, pp. 260-6 are devoted to Spanish monody. Almost exclusively a summary of Anglés's remarks on the music of the *CSM.* Printed excerpts include bits of *cantigas* 139, 166, 207, 59, and 124.

1955

251 Clarke, Dorothy Clotelle, "Versification in Alfonso el Sabio's *Cantigas*", *HR*, XXIII (1955), 83-98.
An important and enlightening study which argues most convincingly that Alfonso, in the metrics of *CSM*, laid the foundation for most of Spanish metrics at large and certainly for all verse forms used before the Siglo de Oro. The range of comments covers metrics, verse forms, strophic patterns, polymetrics, synalepha, hiatus, enjambement, accent, the movable caesura, and the presence of free verse.

252 Fernández Pousa, Ramón, "Cancionero gallego de Bernal de Bonaval", *RDTP*, XI (1955), 478-515.
The pertinent section is entitled "Alfonso X el Sabio, Pero da Ponte y

Bernal de Bonaval", pp. 489-96. It takes up Alfonso's satire of Pero da Ponte in *CV* 68 and 70, and concurs with Costa Pimpão's estimate (1947) that the criticism is levelled because Pero does not use his skill in praise of the Virgin. *CSM* 260 is called upon to lend support to this position. Further demonstration comes from the interpretation given to the final strophe of *cantiga* 10, in which Alfonso himself is a model for such praise. This same stanza might well be a reproof based on a secular variant of the theme in a poem by Bonaval, for it is to Bonaval that Alfonso unfavourably compares Pero da Ponte.

253   Steiger, Arnald, "Las *Cantigas* de Alfonso el Sabio", *Clavileño*, VI, no. 33 (mayo-junio 1955), 14-18.
Cloyingly written in florid prose by a student and follower of Ribera. The article contains a good short study of *CSM* 209. However, the analysis tends to exaggerate the role of personal factors in the explication of the poem's content.

1956

254   Baraut, Cebrià, "Un Recull de miracles de Santa Maria, procedent de Ripoll i les *Cantigues* d'Alfons el Savi", in *Maria-Ecclesia, Regina et Mirabilis* (Scripta et Documenta, VI, Montserrat: Abadia de Montserrat, 1956), pp. 127-60.
Of the 22 Marian miracles in codex Rivipullensis 193, folios 27v-48r, dating from the twelfth and thirteenth centuries, 21 also appear in the *CSM*. While B. admits that this MS is no direct source of Alfonso's accounts of the miracles, there are still enough similarities, especially in the seven dealing with Rocamadour, to indicate a not-too-remote, common Latin source. In the order of their appearance, the Latin analogues B. prints from the Ripoll MS correspond to the *CSM* as follows: 231, 4, 138, 15, 145, 2, 141, 68, 111, 132, 405, 134, 149 (Baraut's 14 does not appear in the *CSM*), 128, and the Rocamadour series − 159, 153, 157, 147, 57, 175, and 158. Nicely done and provocative. Further study of this MS is required.

255   Fernández Pousa, Ramón, "Menéndez y Pelayo y el códice florentino de las *CSM* de Alfonso X el Sabio", *RABM*, LXII (1956), 235-55.
Necessary for students of the Florence MS. Contains a complete index with titles/epigraphs, and gives themes, rhymes, metrical schemes, and summaries of the contents of the miniatures. It uses Valmar's numbers from J.b.2 which can be quickly changed to Mettmann's by consulting vol. I of the latter's edition (1959), pp. xvi-xix, the "E" column. This article complements those of Solalinde (1918) and Aita (1921).

256 Guerrero Lovillo, José, *Miniatura gótica castellana: Siglos XIII a XIV* (Madrid: CSIC, 1956). 42 pp. + 48 plates.
A brief résumé of much that is useful from his *magnum opus* (1949). Plates are accompanied by notes. *CSM* featured in the plates are: 1, 2, 9, 12, 24, 28, 32, 35, 44, 46, 228, 59, 64, 74, 87, 94, 99, 103, 107, 108, 124, 126, 130 (depicting Alfonso), 137-8, 142 (depicting Alfonso), 143-4, 154, 169, 158, and 175. All are from MS T.j.1 (of the Escurial), except for 228 which comes from the Florence MS (*cantiga* 88). The art itself stresses the disposition of material and is eclectic in technique. The artists, Guerrero theorizes, were itinerant, perhaps travelling with Alfonso's court.

257 Martínez Molina, Laura, "Las *CSM* del Rey Alfonso el Sabio", Seminario español, Univ. of Barcelona, tesina no. TL-11, 1956. 57 pp.
Unoriginal, diffuse, and with a very out-of-date bibliographical background. There are chapters on themes, sources, language, versification, and music but none is worth consulting. Four of the *CSM* are glossed, in pairs (66 and 2; 46 and 107), but to no avail. An item best left on the shelf.

258 Roberts, Kimberley S., *An Anthology of Old Portuguese* (Lisbon: Livraria Portugal, n.d. [1956?]).
Includes six Alfonsine poems: a *cantiga d'amor*, *CBN* 413; a *cantiga d'escarnho*, *CBN* 439; and four of the *CSM*, 8, 36, 70, and 103. Lapa's orthography is followed, as distinct from Valmar's. Brief notes on each poem can be found at the end of the volume.

1957

259 Álvarez Blázquez, J.M. "Una réplica literaria de don Enrique el Senador a su hermano Alfonso el Sabio", *Cuadernos de Estudios Gallegos*, XII (1957), 65-91.
Alfonso's well-known disdain for traitors is often vented in the secular *cantigas*, as in *CV* 63, on which a useful comment or two can be found here. This disdain may have extended to Alfonso's brother Enrique, and the analysis of *CV* 61 aims to demonstrate this. The *réplica* is *CV* 3793 (attributed to Enrique) and, even if composed for Enrique by another poet, it is seen as a response to the veiled allusions to fraternal treachery Alfonso writes into *CV* 61.

260 Asensio, Eugenio, *Poética y realidad en el cancionero peninsular de la Edad Media* (Madrid: Gredos, 1957; 2nd ed. 1970).
Alfonso's poetry is treated *passim*. The author contributes the thought

that Alfonso employed a Galician-Portuguese idiom that is hispanically tinged, and suggests that Alfonso was the real founder of the Castilian poetic tradition (p. 96, 1957 ed.). Poems cited are *CBN* 417, 418, and *CSM* 90, 320, 160, and 406, the *mayas.*

261   Domínguez Bordona, Jesús, "Diccionario de iluminadores españoles", *BRAH,* CXL (1957), 49-170.
The brief section, "Iluminadores de Alfonso el Sabio" (pp. 110-11), lists the known artists who worked on Alfonsine MSS. These include, for the *CSM*, Pedro Lorenzo, Juan Pérez, and possibly, Iohannes Gundisalvi.

262   Martins, Mário, "Os *Santos Meninos de Santarém* e os livros de milagres de Nossa Senhora", *Brotéria,* LXV (1957), 555-68. Rpt in *Estudos de cultura medieval,* I (Lisbon: Verbo, 1969), pp. 237-53.
For the sources and analogues of the tale of a child who offers bread to Jesus (or Mary) and is told he will soon be eating of the bread of heaven, this article is extremely valuable since more than a dozen variations are discussed. Relevant Alfonsine poems are *CSM* 139 and 353.

263   Menéndez Pidal, Ramón, *Poesía juglaresca y orígenes de las literaturas románicas: problemas de historia literaria y cultural* (Madrid: Instituto de Estudios Políticos, 1957). viii + 413 pp.
Although the book is greatly enlarged, in some areas, over the original version (see 1924), the sections on Alfonso are insignificantly retouched. Some of the miniatures from J.b.2 are in colour and on better paper.

264   Pereira Tavares, J., ed., *Antologia de textos medievais* (Col. de Clássicos Sá da Costa, Lisbon: Livraria Sá da Costa, 1957; 2nd ed., 1961 [cited]).
Contains, of Alfonso's poetry, *CV* 68-70 (wrongly numbered as 468-70) on pp. 11-14, and *CSM* 103 on pp. 67-70.

265   Schoen, Wilhelm von, *Alfons X, von Kastilien* (Munich: F. Bruckmann, 1957). Trans. into Spanish as *Alfonso X, de Castilla* (Madrid: Rialp "Libros de Bolsillo", 1966).
Pages 84-9 (Spanish version) treat Alfonso briefly as "poeta y trovador". Contained therein is the curious theory about a rival Marian collection in Arabic which may have encouraged writing of the *CSM.* The principal value of the remarks is that of refocussing interest onto the psychological role of the *CSM* in the career, comportment, and artistic values of a poet who also happened to be a ruling monarch.

1958

266   Anglés, Higinio, *La música de las "CSM" del rey Alfonso el Sabio. Facsímil, transcripción y estudio crítico*, III (Barcelona: Diputación Provincial, Biblioteca Central, 1958). In two parts, with 674 pp. of consecutive pagination, plus 98 independently-paginated pp. of musical examples at the end of the second part.

Part One offers full coverage of musical practices in the Peninsula from the very beginning of traceable history. In ch. 3 (pp. 89-139), the poetic courts of Fernando III and Alfonso X are treated with deep scholarly insight. There is an important exposition of musical notation which leads A. to the assertion (the first ever) of how technically consistent are both the Escurial MSS (J.b.2 and T.j.l) in the treatment of mixed modes in their music. Chapter 5 is a brilliant demonstration of the variety of metrical patterns in the *CSM* by the distinguished Romanist Hans Spanke (it is in German but Spanish summaries are later supplied by A.); this ought, in the light of recent work on metrics, to be revised and updated. The *loores* are, for the first time, treated extensively as a subgrouping apart from the more narrative poems and some tentative conclusions about their special variety and technical freedom are given. Other musical types contemporaneous with the *CSM* are evaluated and the volume concludes with a series of tables which further analyse aspects of metrical and musical schemes. In sum, these are studies whose impact cannot be overlooked, even though they are, A. admits, not the final words to be said.

Part Two contains comparative studies of Galician-Portuguese, Italian, Provençal, and French musical cultures. Two pertinent sections are those dealing with the musical miniatures of the *CSM* (pp. 453-7) and with the Virgin Mary in medieval music (pp. 459-81).

The final section, paginated separately, is a kind of anthology of musical examples of all the groups mentioned above as well as some from the *CSM*. The latter include: 60, 78, 93, 97, 108, 112, 115, 129, 134, 138, 141, 150, 157, 161, 162 (two variants), 171, 176-7, 180, 182-3, 187, 196, 203, 206, 210, 212, 239-40, 246, 254, 283, 294, 301, 339-40, 367, 401, and also (I here give A.'s numbers with the corresponding Mettmann nos in parenthesis) from App. I, nos. 2 (412), 5 (415), 6 (416), 10 (420), 11 (421), and, from App. II, 3 (425), 7 (403), 9 (405), and 10 (407).

An extensive bibliography is contained in the voluminous notes. Each chapter has its own bibliography and the items in these are occasionally annotated. For the other vols of this study see 1943 and 1964.

267   Carilla, Emilio, "El Rey de las *Cantigas*", in *Estudios de*

literatura española (Rosario: Univ. Nacional del Litoral, Facultad de Filosofía, Letras y Ciencias de la Educación, 1958), pp. 7-23.
A somewhat disappointing effort. C. inexplicably assumes that it has been generally considered that the *CSM* were the product of Alfonso's youth. Even at this late date, he follows Ribera's Arabist theories and shows that he has not read closely the serious studies which oppose them. He tends to dwell overlong on points, e.g. the use of Galician-Portuguese, that need little discussion, since they have been aired often and at length.

268   Fernández Pousa, Ramón, ed., "Alfonso X, el Sabio: Cantigas de loor de Santa Maria", *Compostellanum*, III (1958), 71-162.
Forty-three *loores* are included, one of which (prol. B) is not a *loor* at all. There is a list of rhyme schemes on p. 76 but in a few cases (*cantigas* 20, 30, 40, 180, 320, and 409) these schemes do not correspond to F.P.'s edition. Poems do not carry numbers. His line numbers do not correspond to those of any other edition, and the frequent use of slash marks makes the poems less readable. No criteria for the edition are ever presented, and F.P. never says which editions of MSS he uses. These and other faults make the work hard to consult. Far easier to use and more reliable overall is Mettmann's edition (1959-72); F.P.'s edition is thus quite expendable. See Rubio Álvarez (1960).

268   Filgueira Valverde, José, "Poesía de santuarios", *Compostella-*
bis   *num*, III (1958), 271-86.
This succinct but wide-ranging survey of medieval Galician sanctuaries as seen through the poetry of the times is very nicely done and of great value. The celebration of both secular and religious activities at the shrines is given full coverage. Alfonsine texts which form an important part of this purview are *CSM* 301, 333, 393, 302, 326, 173, 193, 304, 298, 386, 362, 168, 366, 375, 164, and 317.

269   Keller, John E., "Daily Living as Presented in the *Canticles* of Alfonso the Learned", *Speculum*, XXXIII (1958), 484-9.
The miniatures of the *CSM*, and esp. of Escurial MS T.j.l, get high marks here for what they show of daily life in the thirteenth century. K. reproduces those that accompany *cantigas* 19 and 107. Comments deal more with the actions taking place than the details of the miniatures which are, in any case, there for the reader to see.

270   Martins, Mário, "Lendas portuguesas de aparições de Nossa Senhora nas *CSM*", *Brotéria*, LXVII (1958), 5-11. Rpt. in *Estudos de cultura medieval*, I (Lisbon: Verbo, 1969), pp. 229-36.

This retelling of the events of *CSM* 237, 245, 399, 333, and 267 is informative and instructive. While no great historical burdens are placed on the "proofs" these poems provide, they do give a greater reality to the roles of such religious lyrics in the fabric of every-day life in the Peninsula. Alfonso's narrative is compared to a similar account in the *Crónicas dos sete primeiros reis de Portugal.*

271   Starkie, Walter Fitzwilliam, "Alfonso the Wise, Minstrels and Troubadours", in *Spain: A Musician's Journey through Time and Space*, I (Geneva: Éditions René Kister, 1958), pp. 31-40.
A brief and impressionistic account in which S. states that the *CSM* were popular songs and employed borrowed melodies. Records accompany the text and the *cantiga* used as recorded illustration is *CSM* 353. The author draws a deft, composite portrait of the famed courtesan, Maria Balteira, in which she attains a three-dimensionality almost unique among the treatments she receives from other critics.

1959

271   Buesa, Jaime, "La música de las *Cantigas*", *San Jorge*
bis   (Barcelona), no. 36 (oct. 1959), 60-7.
The title is slightly misleading. This article is occasioned by the publication of Anglés's vols (1958) on the music of the *CSM*, but features a short history of the "Sección de Música" of the Diputación de Barcelona and mention of its other publications. There is an appreciation of Anglés's role in the recovery and actualization of much early music of Spain and, in particular, the music of the *CSM*. A summary of the contents of A.'s recent volumes is offered, without discussion.

272   Keller, John E., "Folklore in the *Cantigas* of Alfonso el Sabio", *Southern Folklore Quarterly*, XXIII (1959), 175-83.
K. establishes that many folkloric themes are present in the *CSM* through the inclusion of traditional tales such as those of *cantigas* 42 and 74. He considers tales of a more local provenance as prime material for Alfonso and his collaborators in the reworking of folk motifs, e.g. *cantigas* 18, 107, and 315. What is lacking here, I think, is a clearer line of demarcation between the folkloric motif used, as it were, subconsciously, and the recording of daily events and homely details which are more properly *costumbrista* in nature. Still, this is one of the first discussions of folklore in the *CSM* and is worth consulting; it could be the starting point for more extensive explorations.

273   ——— , "King Alfonso's Virgin of Villa-Sirga, Rival of St James of Compostela", in *Middle Ages-Reformation-Volkskunde: Festschrift for John G. Kunstmann* (Chapel Hill: Univ. of

North Carolina Press, 1959), pp. 75-81.

A claim is made – through the examples of *CSM* 218, 253, and 278 – that Alfonso may be responsible for originating the decline of the cult of Santiago in Spain. In each of these poems Santa Maria de Vila-Sirga (to whom fourteen *cantigas* are dedicated) is the beneficiary of such a decline. In Alfonso's time, her cult was flourishing grandly. Generally the texts will support K.'s thesis, except, I believe, in his concluding remarks on *cantiga* 253.

274   —— , "The Motif of the Statue Bride in the *Cantigas* of Alfonso the Learned", *Studies in Philology*, LVI (1959), 453-8.

K. presents *CSM* 42 and briefly summarizes its story line. Pages 454-5 list many medieval and modern analogues of the tale, although there is space only for a discussion of one – that of William of Malmesbury.

275   Mettmann, Walter, ed., *Cantigas de Santa Maria*, 4 vols (Coimbra: Acta Universitatis Conimbrigensis, 1959-72). lxxxvii + 287, 379, 415, and 325 pp.

This is the only wholly reliable edition of the poetic texts of the complete *CSM*, with Escurial MS J.b.2 serving as the base (Valmar, 1889, used the same base MS), and including all the additional poems from the Toledo and Florence MSS as well. Variants come from these MSS and also from Escurial T.j.l. The introd. has excellent descriptions of all four, a matching list of the contents of each, the criteria used in this edition, and a splendid and complete Index (with composition numbers, epigraphs and refrains for all the poems). The poems occupy vols I-III; IV consists of a complete glossary with contextual meanings and locations cited but without etyma. This edition is indispensable for all work on the *CSM*.

1960

276   Anglés, Higinio, "Marie dans le chant liturgique et dans la poésie lyrique chantée du Moyen Âge", in *Maria et Ecclesia. Acta Congressus Mariologici-Mariani in civitate Lourdes anno 1958 celebrati* (Rome: Academia Mariana Internationalis, 1960), pp. 331-42.

These particular pages deal with the topic "Maria et ars religiosa" and they outline rather than specify the presence of Mary in liturgical song. In addition collections in Latin and the vernaculars are also brought into the discussion. A. feels that the *CSM* may well have to be considered the greatest single medieval Marian collection.

277   Holliday, F.R., "The Relations Between Alfonso X and Pero

da Ponte", *Revista da Faculdade de Letras* (Lisbon), 3rd series, IV (1960), 152-64.

A full and rather speculative discussion which leans heavily on Michaëlis de Vasconcellos (1904), Menéndez Pidal (1924), and De Lollis (1925). Under discussion are Alfonso's *CV* 68 and 70 in which he criticizes Pero da Ponte. There is here a surprising omission (Bertoni, 1923) which renders the articles less useful than it would have otherwise been. However, the author, if he has not read Bertoni, nevertheless comes to practically the same conclusion. The merit of this article is that H. broaches more aspects of the literary relations between the two poets.

278   Iglesia Alvariño, Aquilino, "La *Cantiga* 202 de Alfonso el Sabio", *Museo de Pontevedra*, XIV (1960), 143-51.

A patriotic effort to suggest the identity of the "arcidiago" of *CSM* 202 with one Adán Fernández (d. 1232?), a Galician. He is sometimes listed as Archdeacon of Santiago on contemporary documents. The dates are right and the conjecture ventured here seems a safe one. Another attempt to see historical accuracy behind the *cantigas* with Peninsular locales.

279   Keller, John E., "Daily Living as Revealed in King Alfonso's *Cantigas*", *KFLQ*, VII (1960), 207-11.

Reproduces a miniature page (in black and white) for *cantiga* 42 – from Escurial MS. T.j.l – and gives an account of the items and activities depicted thereupon. See also his 1959 study of this same *cantiga*, on the motif of the statue-bride.

280   Keller, John E., and Robert W. Linker, "Some Spanish Summaries of the *CSM*", *RoN*, II (1960-1), 63-7.

The authors draw attention to the Castilian prose notes in the margins of the first 25 *CSM* in Escurial MS T.j.l. The only one reproduced here is *cantiga* 24 (both the Galician poetic text and the Castilian prose). The prose seems to have been supplied from some independent source since the order of events, the changes in emphasis, and the additions and omissions will not support the idea that it is a translation of the verse text as given (of this *cantiga*, at least). See also the same authors' 1975 article and Chatham (1976) for further work on these prose pieces.

281   London, Gardiner, "Bibliografía de estudios sobre la vida y obra de Alfonso X el Sabio", *Boletín de Filología Española*, no. 6 (abril, 1960), 18-31.

For its time, this bibliography represented an extensive effort to bring together works of diverse nature on Alfonso and his writings. It complements and updates Sánchez Pérez's works (1933, 1935, and 1944) but does not supersede them in volume of bibliographical material. London omits many contributions, some of them important; a few of his entries have proved untraceable.

282   Pellegrini, Silvio, "Una *cantiga de maldizer* di Alfonso X (*B* 476)", *Studi Mediolatini e Volgari*, VIII (1960), 165-72.
P. deals with *CB* 370, "Non quer'eu donzela fea". He takes up similar poems from the Portuguese *cancioneiros* and adds ample detail and documentation to the more scabrous elements and images of the courtly parody as it was presented by Alfonso in this poem. Shows that Alfonso was a poet working within a conscious tradition.

283   Rubio Álvarez, Fernando, O.S.A. "Observaciones a la edición de una breve antología de las *Cantigas* de Alfonso el Sabio", *Ciudad de Dios*, CLXXIII (1960), 327-33.
A comment on the edition by Fernández Pousa (1958) of the Alfonsine *loores*; rightly says it does not deserve to be called critical. Includes a list of errors but does not catch them all. The author would like to see the eleven compositions denoted as "festas" included among the *loores* (a suggestion which surely deserves some further consideration). There is a note, the only reference I have seen, alluding to an edition of the *CSM* under preparation by Dámaso Alonso and to be published in Barcelona.

284   Torres Fontes, Juan, *La cultura murciana en el reinado de Alfonso X* (Murcia: Academia Alfonso X el Sabio, 1960). 37 pp.
A succinct and useful study, which deals with the *CSM* on pp. 20-37. It not only summarizes the role of the city and realm of Murcia in the *CSM*, but also links, credibly, in one enterprise, the diverse personalities of Pedro Lourenço (*CSM* 377), the poet-musician Bonamic (*CSM* 375), and Ramón de Rocafull (*CSM* 382), all of whom have connections with Murcia. Torres Fontes continues to relate other personalities of Alfonso's court – Maria Balteira, Pedr'Amigo, Ponç, Guiraut Riquier, Fray Pedro Gallego, and Pedro Gómez Barroso – to events and happenings in Murcia. His background as an historian and his judicious speculation make for a refreshingly confident approach to the factual panorama that the Alfonsine texts offer. More work of this quality is needed on the factual background of the local Iberian miracles of the *CSM* in order to better assess the efforts and motives of Alfonso.

1961

285   Lapesa, Rafael, "¿Amor cortés o parodia? A propósito de la primitiva lírica de Castilla", *Estudis Romànics*, IX (1961),

11-14. Rpt. in *De la Edad Media a nuestros días: estudios de historia literaria* (Madrid: Gredos, 1967), pp. 48-52.

Alfonso's sole poem in Castilian, an apparent fragment, is *CB* 363. To L.'s mind it represents a parody and a means to avoid composing true love lyrics, an activity which would have diluted somehow the warlike psychology fomented by martial epics. Parody of true love lyrics, it is contended, is more consistent with this frame of mind. Interesting theory built on a minimal sample.

286 Pellegrini, Silvio, "Pero da Ponte e il provenzalismo di Alfonso X", *AION-SR*, III (1961), 127-37.

P. reviews the critical debate concerning Alfonso's *cantiga de maldizer*, *CV* 70, and rejects all the previous commentary (Michaëlis de Vasconcellos, Rodrigues Lapa, De Lollis, Bertoni, Nunes, and Costa Pimpão) which assumes that Alfonso is critical of his fellow poet Pero da Ponte. On the contrary, the poetic stance is just good, clean fun, part of a game initiated in a *partimen* poem debated between Garcia Martinz and Pero da Ponte (*CV* 1652). This article is characterized by original thinking and sheds interesting new light on the topic. Some shortcomings are discussed by M.M.M. de Oliveira in *Boletim de Filologia*, XXI (1962-3), 153-4. See also Panunzio's ed. of P. da P. (1967).

1962

287 [Alfonso X, el Sabio] "Cantiga 340 de loor a Santa Maria" (Pontevedra: Museo de Pontevedra, Hogar Provincial, 1962). 2 leaves, 1 plate.

A commemorative program featuring the lovely Cousiño woodcut of the Virgin as the "Divina Peregrina" used to illustrate the text of *CSM* 340, a *loor* in the tradition of medieval dawn song.

288 Anglés, Higinio, "Les cantigues Montserratines del rei Alfons el Savi i la seva importància musical", in *Miscellànea Anselm Maria Albareda* (Montserrat: Abadia de Montserrat, 1962), pp. 19-32.

A. publishes new musical transcriptions for the six Montserrat *cantigas: CSM* 48, 52, 57, 113, 302, and 311. The versions edited by Sunyol (1924), and which had been transcribed by Anglés's teacher Friedrich Ludwig, are not faithful enough to the Alfonsine MSS. Since all six have *virelai* melodies, similar to Catalan folk dance songs of the thirteenth century, A. wonders whether he ought to conclude that this is a felicitous coincidence or, perhaps, a deliberate occurrence. He is right to do so. In addition to the faithful transcriptions there is a facsimile of the music, text, and the miniatures of *CSM* 52 from Escurial MS T.j.l.

289 Domínguez Bordona, Jesús, "Manuscritos alfonsíes y franco-góticos de Castilla, Navarra y Aragón", *Ars Hispaniae*, XVIII (Madrid: Ed. Plus Ultra, 1962), pp. 111-29, esp. 111-18.
Deft and informative resumé of what, very generally, is known of the manuscript art of the *CSM* MSS. One of the Escurial MSS belonged, it is suggested, to Isabel la Católica. The style seems to reveal a freedom of interpretation given the artists in the portrayal of their subjects. The author believes that the artists were local Iberian personalities trained in the techniques of French illumination. Six miniatures are reproduced, one in colour.

290 Fernandes Lopes, Francisco, "Ainda as *Cantigas de Santa Maria*", in *Congresso luso-espanhol para o progresso das ciências* (Oporto, 1962), pp. 409-11.
A sequel to two articles on the music of the *CSM* (1965, 1968). The author refers to his own system of notation in which fourteen of the *CSM* were performed in Oporto in 1952. By now he has had ample time to study and assess Anglés's contributions to the field. He declares them satisfactory but feels they are still not fully definitive. Since he does not state why they fall short, it will take more than this brief assessment to bring down the considerable edifice of musicological scholarship so carefully and diligently constructed by Anglés over many years.

291 Martínez Alfonso, Manuel, "Alfonso X y las *Cantigas* a Santa Maria", in *El Puerto de Santa María en la literatura española: Ensayo de una geografía literaria* (Puerto de Santa María: Medusa, 1962), pp. 63-73.
This minor study mentions the 24 *CSM* whose locale is Puerto de Santa María (328, 356-9, 364, 366-8, 371-2, 375-9, 381-2, 385, 389, 391-3, and 398) and, in essence, adheres closely to the findings of Sancho de Sopranís (1935, not seen; but see below for 1964, a study in which some of the earlier ideas are repeated) and of J. Cabello (1909). The author is given to little more than paraphrase, but since both studies are hard to find, he performs a useful service, especially in discussion of *cantigas* 367 and 328.

292 Menéndez Pidal, Gonzalo, "Los manuscritos de las *Cantigas*: Cómo se elaboró la miniatura alfonsí", *BRAH*, CL (1962), 25-51.
An invaluable study of the *CSM* codices which are minutely described and compared. The Florence MS is shown, rather convincingly, to be both the often cited codex once in the possession of J. Lucas Cortés

and the second part of the truncated Escurial MS T.j.l. The incomplete state of the illumination process of the Florence codex provided the author with the basis for the description of a reasonable seven-step procedure by which the Alfonsine artists created the *CSM* miniatures. Then, granting the possibility of French, Italian, and even Germanic illumination styles, M.P. compares two illustrations from a 1237 copy of al-Hariri's *Maqāmat* with *CSM* 185 l and 165 k (from T.j.l), a comparison which shows, to the author's satisfaction, the influence of Arabic miniature style on Alfonso's very diverse artists. He adduces, furthermore, the names of six of the artists (and scribes) who doubtless shared in the great artistic enterprise of the *CSM*.

293   Mettmann, Walter, "Lexicalisches und Etymologisches aus den *CSM*", *Romanische Forschungen*, LXXIV (1962), 31-59. In anticipation of vol. IV of the ed. of the *CSM* (not published until 1972), M. prints some 180 of the more unusual lexical items to be encountered in Alfonso's work. Since this long article includes etymologies as well as discussions, it is more valuable than the corresponding entries in the 1972 vol., which does not. Contextual citations are also more generous here.

294   Nemésio, Vitorino, ed., *A poesia dos trovadores. Antologia.* (Lisbon: Livraria Bertrand, n.d. [1962?]), pp. 91-9. The general introduction is fair. Poems by Alfonso are *CSM* 1, 10, 70, and 406, and *CV* 77.

295   Pellegrini, Silvio, "Arnaut (Catalan?) e Alfonso X di Castiglia", *Bollettino del Centro di Studi Filologici e Linguistici Siciliani*, VII (*Saggi e ricerche in memoria di Ettore Li Gotti*, II: 1962), 480-6. P. suggests some connection between *CB* (MS) 477 of Alfonso and the quite similar *partimen* between Arnaut Catalan and a variously identified Midi count. Points of contact are the risqué theme and the malicious tone. Problems which P. cannot resolve are many: the identity of the two antagonists, Arnautz and Arnaldo, as the same person, the accurate dating of the two compositions, and the nature of the events referred to. Interesting but not conclusive.

296   ———— , "Le due laude alfonsine del canzoniere Colocci-Brancuti", in *Romania: Scritti offerti a Francesco Piccolo nel suo LXX compleanno* (Naples: Armanni Ed., 1962), pp. 359-68. P. edits *CB* (MS) 467 and 468. The first is also *CSM* 40; the second seems to be the first stanza of another, unknown Alfonsine *loor*. Both indicate that Alfonso probably composed religious verse earlier than

had been supposed by most critics, both being out of place here among his secular, and sometimes quite profane, poetry. P. feels his edition of *CB* 467/*CSM* 40 offers readings preferable to those of either Valmar (1889) or Mettmann (1959). For *CB* 468, he clears up some readings of the Machado ed. (1949) which made parts of this surviving 8-line strophe unintelligible.

1963

297   Ballesteros y Beretta, Antonio. *Alfonso X el Sabio* (Barcelona: Salvat Editores, and Murcia: CSIC, Academia "Alfonso X el Sabio", 1963). xv + 1142pp. + 28pp. of plates.
The fullest biography and the best. Lack of an index hampers the user. However, students of Alfonsine poetry will find, usually in an historical context, curious notes on *cantigas* 221 (pp. 16-17), 169 and 328 (pp. 279-80, 332), 328 alone (p. 283), 354, 366, 376, and 377 (pp. 299-305), Prol. A and 183 (pp. 319-20), 325 (p. 588), 323 (pp. 761-3), 235 (pp. 771, 787-9, and 811), 300 (p. 777), 215 and 406 (pp. 834-5), and 386 (pp. 951-3). *CV* 77 and 79 are discussed briefly on pp. 813-14 and there is a section entitled "La corte y los juglares" on pp. 345-56. Maria Balteira appears on p. 381 and much contemporary praise of Alfonso as poet and protector of poets is quoted on pp. 503-8.

298   Bertolucci, Valeria, "Contributo allo studio della letteratura miracolistica", in *Miscellanea di studi ispanici* (Istituto di Letteratura Spagnola e Ispano-Americana dell'Università di Pisa, Pubblicazioni, VI, Pisa, 1963), pp. 5-72.
A splendid exposition and required reading for several reasons: the thorough discussion of realism in Latin and vernacular miracle literature; the elucidation of how full of art are the purportedly simple styles of Gautier de Coincy, Berceo and Alfonso X (generous space being devoted to the latter); the sensitive discussion of the concept of originality in this genre accompanied by a fine exposition of Gregory the Great and his followers; and the cogent appraisal of Alfonso's artistic method in selected *cantigas* (*CSM* 79, 47, 4, 289, 325, 254, 317, and 279).

299   Mettmann, Walter, "Stand und Aufgaben der Alfonsinischen Forschungen", *Romanistisches Jahrbuch*, XIV (1963), 269-93.
The relevant section is on pp. 287-93. Here M. deals with studies on varied aspects of Alfonsine poetry and offers comments and suggestions for topics of future study. Especial emphasis is given to the area of metrics and its relations with musical patterns.

300   ——— , "Zwei Wörter aus den *CSM*", *Archiv für das Studium der Neueren Sprachen und Literaturen*, CXCIX (1962-3),

99-100.
Word histories for 'vargallon' (*CSM* 227) and 'combo' (*CSM* 39).

1964

301 Anglés, Higinio, *La música de las "CSM" del Rey Alfonso el Sabio. Facsímil, transcripción y estudio crítico*, I (Barcelona: Diputación Provincial de Barcelona, Biblioteca Central, 1964). xvi + 12 pp + 361 folios.
This (vol. I of the work though the last to appear in print) is the only complete facsimile ed. of Escurial MS J.b.2 and concludes Angles's great work on the music of the *CSM*. It is from this MS that Anglés made his musical transcriptions (1943), the study of which was completely published later (1958). The copy is unusually clear.

302 Nelson, Charles Leslie, "Literary and Pictorial Treatment of the Devil in the *CSM*", unpubl. M.A. thesis, Univ. of North Carolina, Chapel Hill, North Carolina, 1964, 164 pp.
A small study made interesting, in part, by the author's inclusion of 86 of his own professional sketches of miniatures from Escurial MS T.j.l. Several points of artistic interest are made in comments on the variety of artists undeniably present in the MS artwork, the concentration of effort to depict detail, and the effort observed in the creation of a gallery of devil-figures. Three-dimensionality and even animation seem to have been intended by these artists. Thirty-eight of the *CSM* are mentioned but text and illustration are lacking for *cantiga* 111 (ch. V). Also comments the divergences between the story told in the poem and the accompanying miniature.

303 Sancho de Sopranís, Hipólito, *Historia de Jerez de la Frontera desde su incorporación a los dominios cristianos*, I: *1255-1492* (Jerez de la Frontera: Editorial Jerez Industrial, 1964), pp. 24-31, 116.
Discussion of the fact and the fiction involved in *CSM* 345 (pp. 24-9), and a note on the founding and rededication as a Christian settlement of the town of Santa María del Puerto (as seen in *CSM* 328). Includes, too, a mention (p. 116, n. 1) of the historicity of *CSM* 374. The author devoted most of his life to the history of Jerez and nearly all his writings highlight Alfonso's role in its early history (24 of the *CSM* are centered in or around the activity of Santa María del Puerto).

1965

304 [Alfonso el Sabio and others] *Cantigas de Santa Maria—El Cantar de los cantares—Sonetos—Coplas que hizo por la*

muerte de su padre D. Rodrigo (Madrid: Ed. Mediterráneo, 1965, 2nd ed. 1969), pp. 9-55.

Twelve of the *CSM* are represented by either complete or partial Spanish translations. I indicate, since the editor does not do so, the number of each according to Mettmann (1959). Translations are complete unless accompanied by strophe numbers in parentheses:

1. 31	5. 98	9. 206 (7, 9)
2. 16	6. 72 (10, 11)	10. 56 (5, 6)
3. 94	7. 286	11. 357
4. 34 (6, 7)	8. 325 (1, 17)	12. 201 (12, 13)

305 Dronke, Peter, *Medieval Latin and the Rise of European Love-Lyric. I. Problems and Interpretations* (Oxford: Clarendon Press, 1965), pp. 52-3, 186.

D. doubts a direct relationship between the stanzaically-similar *zéjel* and the *rondeau* (and *virelai*). He supports the proposition that Alfonso borrowed the form from the Arabic South: it was an accustomed form which had been nourished for a long time in the Peninsula. In his discussion of the medieval use of the *flos florum* conceit, he brings in *CSM* 10 (p. 186). The entire book is worth concentrated reading, even if Alfonso's part in it is small.

306 Pérez de Urbel, Dom Justo, "Un gallego que nació en Toledo, Rey Sabio, y poeta principal", *Estafeta Literaria*, nos. 320-1 (1965), 20-1.

A chauvinistic overview of Alfonso and his poetry which is too frequently inaccurate. Nothing here is particularly new, if one excepts the licence permitting the author to class Alfonso as a real "gallego".

307 Rodrigues Lapa, Manuel, *Cantigas d'escarnho e de mal dizer dos cancioneiros medievais galego-portugueses* (Colección Filolóxica, Vigo: Editorial Galaxia, 1965; 2nd ed. 1970, revista e acrescentada).

Critical edition of 35 of Alfonso's satirical poems (nos 1-35; for corresponding numbers in other editions, see my Appendix A) and of four of the *tensons* with other poets (nos 150, 305, 422, and 430 in the 1970 ed.; in the 1965 ed., nos are 149, 303, 419, and 427). All have comprehensive historical and literary notes with explication of contents, variants, and, especially useful, summaries of prior critical controversy (when applicable). A separate 108-page vocabulary (non-etymological), and the author, first line, and onomastic indices enhance the utility of this excellent, long-needed edition of these Alfonsine texts.

308 ——— , *Miscelânea de língua e literatura portuguesa medieval*

(Rio de Janeiro: Inst. Nacional do Livro, 1965), pp. 198-201. The entire book deals with matters tangential to Alfonso X as poet and these specific pages berate Mussafia (1895) for his forced interpretations of metrics affecting many of the *CSM*.

1966

309   Bertolucci Pizzorusso, Valeria, "La supplica di Guiraut Riquier e la risposta di Alfonso X di Castiglia", *Studi Mediolatini e Volgari*, XIV (1966), 9-135.
Excellent, readable editions of the two poems (both by Riquier) with translations into Italian prose. Good notes. A list of terms from the poems that are oriented to art and artistry serves as a fine introduction. Also treated is the question of whether a similar *supplicatio-declaratio* between Alfonso and N'At de Mons (both set down, also in Provençal, by the latter) ever took place. The poetic background and the period of composition are reflected and there is criticism of the earlier studies by Michaëlis de Vasconcellos (1896) for not carrying enough etymological information. Many themes are treated in this long and trustworthy contribution to Alfonsine scholarship, and they give a clear view of the thirteenth-century poetic milieu. See also Vuolo (1968).

310   Fisher, John H., ed., *The Medieval Literature of Western Europe: A Review of Research, Mainly 1930-1960* (MLA Revolving Fund Series, XXII, New York: New York Univ. Press for Modern Language Assoc. of America, and London: Univ. of London Press, 1966), pp. 330-40, 374, 377.
Far too little of the research available on Alfonsine poetry is reported on here, either in the Spanish section or the Portuguese.

311   Mettmann, Walter, "Zu Text und Inhalt der altportugiesischen *Cantigas d'escarnho e de mal dizer*", *ZRP*, LXXXII (1966), 308-19.
Extensive comments occasioned by Rodrigues Lapa's ed. (1965); more were promised but, to my knowledge, they have not appeared. However, since the edition began with Alfonso X, Alfonsine scholars can profit from M's shrewd observations, and from some few doubts on certain readings and suggested alternate readings, as well as interpretations and clarifications for *cantigas* 5, 11, 13, 14, 22, 23, and 29 (R.L.'s numbering).

312   Pedrell, Felipe, *Cuatro cantigas. XXVIII. LX. LXI. LXV* (Madrid: Unión Musical Española, 1966). 9 pp.
Sheet music for four of the six *CSM* transcribed by P. in 1905 and possibly earlier.

1967

313   Foster, David W., "Medieval Poetic Tradition in Two *Cantigas profanas* of Alfonso el Sabio", *RoN*, VIII (1966-7), 297-304.
Neither of the poems F. comments is really profane (secular), as both belong to the *CSM* (406 and 60), and both are devotional and center on Mary. Also, too much is read into the *mayas* (406). Rather than the figural motif, this *cantiga* depends on the simple belief, often sung, that "May is Mary's Month". While pagan memories of May-days are latent, it seems an overinterpretation to give them such priority in what is essentially an incantatory *cantiga* whose litaneutical imitation is built on sound-plays on May/Mary. In *CSM* 60, Eve and Mary are joined in figural union but the whole poem is structured around repetitions of contrasts, mirror images (e.g. the AVE/EVA topos), and oppositions. Such considerations are not given their due.

314   García Gómez, Emilio, "Quince cantigas de escarnio galaico-portuguesas", *Revista de Occidente*, new series, XVIII (1967), 181-99.
These are free translations into Castilian. Two, nos 1 and 15, are Alfonso's *CB* (MS) 480 and 491, respectively.

315   Keller, John E., *Alfonso X, el Sabio* (Twayne World Author Series, XII, New York: Twayne, 1967). 198 pp.
Written primarily for the lay reader, this volume covers almost all phases of Alfonso's career and literary output. Ch. 5 deals with the *CSM* and ch. 6 with the secular poems. Topics treated briefly are Alfonso's personal involvement in the writing of the *CSM*, the reflection of daily living seen in selected texts and miniatures (*cantiga* 157 gets full treatment), versification schemes (modelled on the previous work of Clarke [1955]), and the music of the songs (based on Anglés's work of 1943 and 1958). *Cantigas* singled out for discussion are 74, 29, and 107. K. also offers translations for sections of Prol. B and *cantiga* 169.
The pages devoted to the profane poems offer less total coverage. Alfonso composed 46 secular poems, in whole or in part (see Tavani [1967]), but K. states there are scarcely more than thirty (p. 96). There are English translations of *CV* 75 and *CB* (MS) 456 (in full) and of *CV* 64, 76 and 69 (in part). There are also partial translations for two works which are in the *CSM*, nos 40 (*CBN* 409) and 406 (the claim that the latter translation is a full one is in error [pp. 108-9]). Alfonso's only Castilian poem, the fragment of *CBN* 414, is also translated. K. is right to stress Alfonso's versatility as a poet.

316   Orbón, Julián, *Tres cantigas del rey* (New York: Franco

Colombo, Inc., 1967). 20 pp.

CSM 65 and 134 are transcribed for soprano, harpsichord, two violins, viola and cello; *CSM* 133 is transcribed for soprano, harpsichord, tenor drum, cymbals, violin, viola, and cello. Performance time for the three should be approximately ten minutes.

317   Panunzio, Saverio, "Le poesie storiche – Rapporti poetici tra Pero da Ponte e Alfonso X", in his ed. of *Pero da Ponte. Poesie* (Biblioteca di Filologia Romanza, X, Bari: Adriatica Editrice, 1967), pp. 43-59, esp. pp. 52-59.

P. uses previous scholarship wisely, especially Pellegrini (1961), whom he follows closely. In reviewing the criticisms Alfonso made of Pero da Ponte in *CV* 68 and 70, P. shows that such displays were part of contemporary poetic play and, like Baena's insults to his friend and teacher Villansandino, not to be taken too literally. Earlier critics interpreted these poems without understanding the spirit of fun which was an integral part of this poetic genre.

318   Tavani, Giuseppe, *Repertorio metrico della lirica galego-portoghese* (Officina Romanica, VII, Rome: Edizioni dell' Ateneo, 1967). 520 pp.

An outstanding achievement, T.'s exhaustive catalogue of the metrical and stanzaic patterns of the poems of *CA*, *CV*, and *CB* (and a few other less abundant MSS) will be, for its subject, the scholarly *vademecum*. The 46 secular poems of Alfonso are most easily located through the Index of Poets on pp. 386-90. From there, one proceeds directly to information regarding the intricacies of their metrical and stanzaic schemes, poetic types, rhymes, and more. This information is in an abbreviated notation and a thorough reading of the introduction – in Italian – is essential. Several indices add to the voluminous information contained, for the first time, between the covers of one book.

1968

319   Bagby, Albert Ian, Jr , "The Moor and the Jew in the *Cantigas* of Alfonso X, el Sabio", unpubl. diss., Univ. of Kentucky, 1968. 208 pp. An abstract appears in *DAI*, XXX (1969-70), 1550-1A.

A shade too eager to accept the *CSM* as evidence of Alfonso's personal attitude toward Moor and Jew. The claim that despite Alfonso's fame as a tolerant monarch he was "in reality quite prejudiced" does not really convince. There is a lack of critical balance (for example, Castro's theories are never questioned, despite the many doubts raised by other serious scholars) and there is no sound discussion of the psychological complexities that such theories are bound to raise. Not enough space is devoted to the consideration that the figures in some of the *Cantigas* are mere literary stereotypal enemies of Mary and Christ and that exaggerated portraits of Jews and Moors need not be the basis for conclusions about Alfonso's personal tastes. B.'s view is interesting and ought to be aired; however, the case for it is not proven here.

320 Colao, Alberto, *El Marqués de Valmar; semblanza bio-biblio-gráfica; sus estudios de las "Cantigas"*, 2nd ed. (Cartagena: Athenas Ed., 1968). 74 pp.
I have not seen the first ed., 1966. The work's value lies mainly in C.'s account of the inception, carrying out, and eventual reception of the 1889 ed. of the *CSM* under the general editorship of Valmar. There are many quotations from the edition's introduction. The ceremony at which this piece was read, in Cartagena, was embellished by the musical performance of several *cantigas*: Prol. B., 65, 69, 21, 26, 10, 169, and 339.

321 Dronke, Peter, *The Medieval Lyric* (London: Hutchinson, 1968), pp. 70-2, 222-4.
On pp. 70-2 we learn that Arabs and Jews helped to compose some of the *CSM* melodies, a debatable point, and that the refrains of the *cantigas* were sung (and danced) after each strophe, also a debatable point (see Cummins, 1970). The observation that Alfonso's tone is often comparable to that which Boccaccio achieves in the *novelle* is a good one. On pp. 222-4 there is a high literary valuation of *CV* 63 which D. thinks is Alfonso's finest song: it is both symbolist and highly original. D. gives the Galician-Portuguese text and his own splendid translation of it.

322 Filgueira Valverde, José, "Aucto 'De como Santa Maria foi levada aos ceos pra a festa de Nosa Señora de Agosto' refeito con testos galegos dos séculos XIII e XIV", *Grial*, XXV (1968), 325-40.
The *aucto* referred to was produced in 1966 and in it are artfully intertwined a prose text from the fourteenth-century *Miragres de Santiago* and sections of *CSM* 419 and 420. The common theme is the Virgin's Assumption. An acting version, in Galician, is printed here.

323 Isorna, A., "Dos melodías de la Virgen peregrina", *Museo de Pontevedra*, XXII (1968), 97-100.
This is a musical transcription of *CSM* 49 ("La Peregrina") which was first made in 1964 as one small offering of the city of Pontevedra to the Santiago Holy Year celebrations of 1965.

324 Mettmann, Walter, "Die altportugiesische Marienlyrik vor 1300", in *Grundriss der romanischen Literaturen des Mittelalters*, vol. VI, ed. H.R. Jauss, part 1 (Heidelberg: Carl Winter, 1968), pp. 15-18.

An expert condensation by an expert. Telling remarks on the structure and evolution of the "editions" of the *CSM*, with J.b.2 as the final one of the series. M. expounds the value of the *loores* to the whole: they best translate the personal emotion of Alfonso as revealed in it. Primary among these are *CSM* 100, 350, 180, 360, 130, 220, 260, 10, 60, 70, 290, and 330. Bibliography is given in vol. VI, part 2 (1970), pp. 43-5.

325 Piel, Joseph M., "Coteifes orpelados, panos d'arrazes e martinhos", *Revista Portuguesa de Filologia*, XIV (1966-8), 1-12.

This dense study deals with *CV* 74. Not satisfied with Rodrigues Lapa's 1965 revisions of Michaëlis de Vasoncellos's 1901 text, P. delves into specific meanings for four unclear terms: 'coteifes', 'orpelados', 'panos d'arrazes', and 'martinhos'. His solutions and suggestions are probably all very near the mark, except the last one, where two hypotheses seem equally engaging.

326 Tavani, Giuseppe, "La cantiga d'escarnho e de mal dicer galego-portoghese", in *Grundriss der romanischen Literaturen des Mittelalters*, vol. VI, ed. H.R. Jauss, part 1 (Heidelberg: Carl Winter, 1968), pp. 309-13.

A brief but vivid sketch of Alfonso's *cantigas* specifically critical of cowards (including a few troubadours) who would not follow him into battle. T. dates these from the period 1261-5. Bibliography is given in vol. VI, part 2 (1970), pp. 317-19 and 422-4.

327 Vuolo, Emilio, "Per il testo della supplica di Guiraut Riquier ad Alfonso X", *Studi Medievali*, 3rd series, IX (1968), 729-806.

A sequel to Bertolucci Pizzorusso's article (1966). Has five parts: 1) an exposition of the poetic background of Alfonso's era; 2) an appreciation of Bertolucci's edition; 3) a paraphrase of both the *Supplicatio* and the *Declaratio*; 4) a neat explication of the moral content and its implications for the transitional social and cultural age depicted therein; and 5) a philosophical foray into the texts which both emends and extends the readings and judgements of Bertolucci. The appendix to this study is an edition, freshly re-punctuated, which is Vuolo's own view of the two works that he has come to know so thoroughly.

1969

328   Alfau de Solalinde, Jesusa, *Nomenclatura de los tejidos españoles del siglo XIII*, Anejo XIX of the *BRAE* (Madrid: RAE, 1969). 203 pp.
An alphabetical listing of cloths mentioned in thirteenth-century works, including the *CSM*. Contains useful etymologies, definitions, and information about unusual cloths. For example, see under "plumas", a material mentioned in *cantigas* 105 and 122.

329   Davis, William R., Jr, "The Role of the Virgin in the *CSM*", unpubl. diss., Univ. of Kentucky, 1969. 177 pp. An abstract appears in *DAI*, XXXI (1970-1), 383A.
D. offers a classification scheme for the almost 360 miracle narrations of the *CSM*, with fifteen divisions (representing roles of the Virgin) such as "Compassion", "Benevolence", "Teacher", "Adviser", and "Provider". Problems arise in this scheme since so many of the roles overlap significantly. Perhaps it is this that leads D. to conclude – not too surprisingly – that Mary in thirteenth-century Iberia was seen as a very human and three-dimensional figure. For another attempt at classification, see Montoya Martínez (1974).

330   González, Juan, Jr, "La sociedad medieval española reflejada en la obra de Alfonso el Sabio", unpubl. diss., Univ. of Texas, 1969. 316 pp. An abstract appears in *DAI*, XXX (1969-70), 3008A.
Various orders of medieval activity are taken up here, largely through information gleaned from the *Siete partidas* and, less richly, from the remaining Alfonsine works. *CSM* 24, 327, and 75 provide lively illustration for notes on clerical laxity (p. 29) while several show other religious customs (G. relies largely on Callcott [1923] and, in the chapter on nobility, on Guerrero Lovillo [1949]). On games and diversions, discussions include *CSM* 6, 238, 174, 72, 136, and 294, and for the hunt there are illustrations from *cantigas* 352, 142, 243, and a few others. The author could have made better use of the *CSM* than he did and he could have been less derivative and more daring in his catalogues of categories of medieval life.

331   Hill, Kathleen Kulp, "The Three Faces of Eve: Woman in the Medieval Galician-Portuguese *Cancioneiros*", *KRQ*, XVI (1969), 97-107.
A trendily-titled article which features Alfonso as author of "shameless satirical poems" (those famed for their *escarnho*) and which is short on valuable insights into the two Alfonsine citations from *CB* 350 and 370 (pp. 103-4).

332 Lorenzo, Ramón, "Notas sobre léxico gallego-portugués", in
Philologische Studien für Joseph M. Piel (Heidelberg: C.
Winter, 1969), pp. 136-9.
Corrects Neuvonen's (1951) reading of *alfaqui* in *CSM* 108 (see under
'alquime' on p. 138) and comments the use of *alfaraz* in *CV* 74.

333 Márquez Villanueva, Francisco, "La poesía de las *Cantigas*",
Revista de Occidente, 2nd series, XXV (1969), 71-93.
Many of the *CSM* are individually treated here, most in very brief
fashion. Especially pinpointed are *cantigas* 351, 354, 178 (the latter
two for their treatment of children and animals, of which Alfonso is
said to have been very fond), and 205, for its psychological depth of
understanding. The article is discursive and seems to lack a central
theme, preferring to touch diverse topics almost at will. Cases in which
one would expect some argument to be offered include the claims that
Alfonso clearly knew Berceo's poems (p. 72), that Alfonso authored all
of the *CSM* (p. 72, and p. 91, n. 8), and that the miracles themselves are
the sole theme of the compilation, i.e., that other sub-themes do not
form part of it.

334 Mettmann, Walter, "Zur Nasalresonanz im Altportugiesischen", *Philologische Studien für Joseph M. Piel* (Heidelberg:
C. Winter, 1969), pp. 162-5.
A study of the use (and non-use) of the tilde in indicating nasal resonance or its absence. Despite some individual scribal use, the *CSM*
manuscripts permit the conclusion that the lack of a tilde marks the
ebb of nasal resonance and is confirmation of a phonetic reality.

335 Moreno Galván, José M., *Cantigas de Alfonso X, el Sabio*
(Col. Gráficos Españoles, III, Madrid: Ed. Ricardo Aguilera,
1969). 10 plates.
In very large format (several times actual size), here are 10 colour plates,
based on Escurial MS T.j.l, corresponding to *CSM* 1, 25, 28, 33, 35, 56,
63, 108, 144, and 183. A brief text by M.G. repeats the absurd claim of
Soriano Fuertes (1855) that the music is in "notación rabínica". There
is, however, much more sense in M.G.'s claim that the tectonic and
linear art of the Alfonsine miniatures, produced probably by a team of
artists, has no peer in its era.

336 Piel, Joseph M., "Zum Text eines Spottlied Alfons des Weisen",
in *Mélanges offerts à Rita Lejeune*, I (Gembloux: J. Duculot,
1969), pp. 503-10.
Piel concentrates on *CV* 65 as printed by Rodrigues Lapa (1965). He
illuminates the problems of interpretation that remain in Alfonso's rich

and involved satiric poems. He scrutinizes the text with care and makes revealing remarks on etymologies, puns, place names, and the like. We are left with a better idea of how well theme and satirical intent complement each other despite some remaining unresolved difficulties.

337   Tavani, Giuseppe, *Poesia del duecento: Problemi del due-cento nella penisola iberica* (Officina Romanica, XII, Rome: Ed. dell'Ateneo, 1969). 292 pp.
Alfonso as poet is treated *passim* (see T.'s Index). Of note are the sensible overview of Alfonso's poetic court (pp. 22-9), some sane comments on the profane poetry (pp. 169-72), and useful notes on a few aspects of rhyme and versification, especially pertaining to *cantiga* 10 (pp. 189-203). Américo Castro's Arabic-tinged reading of the *CSM* (1948) is given very short shrift on pp. 14-18.

1970

338   Bagby, Albert I., Jr, "Alfonso X, el Sabio compara moros y judíos", *RF*, LXXXII (1970), 578-83.
Both Moors and Jews occupy the stage in *CSM* 5, 264, 348, and 401, though only with any real importance in 348. When both appear in the same composition, B. contends that the Jew fares worse than the Moor and, on this kind of evidence, B. would like to conclude that Alfonso was privately less hostile to the followers of Mohammed. It is an interesting idea, but the few texts are statistically insignificant for proof of the author's contention. Furthermore, no additional texts are submitted, nor are any contemporary documents cited to suggest that the flesh-and-blood Alfonso was indeed more favourable to Moors than to Jews. An early version of these same arguments forms part of the author's doctoral dissertation (1968).

339   —— , "Some Characterizations of the Moor in Alfonso X's *Cantigas*", *South Central Bulletin*, XXX (1970), 164-7.
B. wishes to show that Alfonso, despite his reputation for tolerance, was much biassed against the Moors. It is true that they were his opponents in religion and on the battlefield; however, the subjective readings of the forty-four *cantigas* in which Muslims are at least mentioned (*CSM* 28, 185, 215, 325, 186, and 379 are dealt with in some detail) do not, to my mind, convincingly reveal any such privately-harboured resentments. Alfonso comes in for too much credit for the artistic depiction of the Muslims. Too many of the Moors appear in ways not unique to the *CSM*, which suggests greater reliance on fixed or stereotyped delineations of the character of the Moor as renegade than B. concedes. In the long line of Marian miracle literature that

precedes the *CSM*, all manner of Jews, Moors and other "infidels" are traditional enemies of the Virgin and are unfavourably represented, except in their potential roles as converts. Separating this traditional depiction from any Alfonso presents in the *CSM* may well prove impossible.

340 Cummins, John G., "The Practical Implications of Alfonso el Sabio's Peculiar Use of the Zéjel", *Bulletin of Hispanic Studies*, XLVII (1970), 1-9.
A dense, important assessment of Alfonso's usage of the *zéjel* form. C. proves, as conclusively as is now possible, that not all the texts of the *CSM* could have been composed with musical considerations in mind. His evidence includes enjambements, the postponement of a true narrative opening until the second strophe of certain *cantigas* (a development which leaves the *estribillo/cabeza* free to establish a tighter relationship with the first strophe), and recognition of the possibility that the *estribillo* was not always intended for repetition at the end of the *cantiga*. C. has reason, logic, and clarity of exposition on his side.

341 Foster, David William, "The Concept of Mary in Thirteenth-Century Spanish Poetry", in *Christian Allegory in Early Hispanic Poetry* (Studies in Romance Languages, IV, Lexington: Univ. of Kentucky Press, 1970), pp. 105-35.
This is a chapter in F.'s more wide-ranging book in which he reprises his comments from his 1967 article on *CSM* 60 and 406 (pp. 105-7 and in a note on p. 111). The general topic of the chapter is figural *topoi* and Marian prophecies and the discussion is not without value.

342 González-Alegre, Ramón, "Reyes poetas en las cantigas de mal decir", *Revista de Literatura*, XXXIV (1968 [1970]), 69-74.
Not at all scholarly. A poetic evocation of Dinis of Portugal and of his grandfather, Alfonso X. Although citations from *CB* 365, 367 and 370 and from *CV* 79 are given, nothing is really made of them, except, perhaps, to posit that these are poems linked to the *pueblo*.

343 Labajo, Aurelio, Carlos Urdiales and Trini González, eds, *Alfonso X, el Sabio. Antología* (Madrid: Coculsa, 1970). 48 pp.
A brief school anthology. Pages 42-7 compress a discussion of Alfonso's lyric into too little space and claim erroneously that there are 430 *CSM*. Only one *cantiga* is printed (*CSM* 4). Of no scholarly value.

344 Sturm, Sara, "The Presentation of the Virgin in the *CSM*",

Philological Quarterly, XLIX (1970), 1-7.

The main point is evident: medieval society had multiple ways to honour Mary, and the *CSM* demonstrate this amply. S. shows, with remarks that could easily have been amplified, that Alfonso preferred illustrating this variety to following his own definition of 'miraculum' offered in the *Siete partidas.*

345 Teensma, B.N., "Os Judeus na Espanha do século XIII, segundo as *CSM* de Afonso X o Sábio", *Ocidente* (Lisbon), LXXIX (1970), 85-102. A version in Dutch appeared in *Studia Rosenthaliana*, IV, no. 2 for 1970.

T. is forced to conclude that Alfonso is an intolerant anti-semite in the *CSM* and in real life; he cites *cantigas* 2, 426, 415, 419, 27, 305, 5, 264, 149, 312, 109, 85, 108, 12, 6, 34, 286, 4, 25, 89, 107, and 208 to support this claim. There is not the least mention of such considerations as received traditions involving Jews, the guilt traditionally associated with them in the Crucifixion, their having been stereotyped by scores of preceding generations, and their general utility as ready-made antagonists of Christian beliefs. What we need is fact to support the fiction and to aid in separating the art from the life (when that is capable of being clearly perceived). Readers should eye this article with reservations.

1971

346 Alemparte, Jaime Ferreiro, "Fuentes germánicas en las *CSM* de Alfonso X el Sabio", *Grial*, XXXI (1971), 31-62.

This study, collating actual docs relating to Hispano-Germanic relations during the reigns of Fernando III and Alfonso X, speculates on similarities between some of Caesarius of Heisterbach's miracle narrations and others by Alfonso, specifically *CSM* 149, 156, 104, 128, and 208. A. furnishes a feasible and respectable route of diffusion for the former's *Dialogus miraculorum* (as well as for other of his works) and, in doing so, provides the means of probable contact between that collection and the *CSM*. Other *cantigas* dealing with Germany and/or Germans are nos 14, 218, 175, 95 and 42. This is a study which offers more than mere theorizations.

347 Bagby, Albert I., Jr, "The Jew in the *Cantigas* of Alfonso X, el Sabio", *Speculum*, XLVI (1971), 670-88.

The role of the Jew in the *CSM* is that of a hated minority (7 per cent of the poems deal with Jews). Alfonso may have been politically tolerant but, B. argues, he was not so tolerant personally. Jews appear in 30 *cantigas* as arch-enemies of Christianity (occasionally as converts to it as in *CSM* 107, 89, and 133), the devil's disciples, usurers, and traitors.

But the thesis is weakened when one realizes that eight of the thirty compositions were widely-circulated accounts whose outline and content are clearly established and over which Alfonso (or his collaborators) had no control. Further, one must accept, more fully than is now possible to determine, the direct authorship (and approval for the illuminations) of Alfonso for the remaining poems. While the concept of personal intervention has been much discussed, its degree and specific application have not been established firmly enough to support B.'s claims here. *Cantigas* entering into the discussion are: 12, 34, 286, 4, 6, 22, 71, 91, 135, 149, 187, 238, 390, 415, 419, and 426 (Jews as arch-enemies); 109, 3, 108, and 425 (as devil's disciple); 25, 27, 51, 85, and 312 (as usurers); and 2 and 348 (as traitors).

348   Brown, Donna F., "A History of the *Zéjel* in Spanish, Portuguese and Catalan Literatures", Studies in Romance Languages and Literatures, XCVII, Microfilm Series, XXXII, unpubl. diss., Catholic Univ., 1971. An abstract appears in *DAI*, XXXII (1971-2), 2082-3 A.

Alfonso's 281 religious and two profane *zéjeles* form an important part of this thorough study (including a sound review of former research into the area) of what the *zéjel* form really is. The review of theories of origins is especially worth consulting: it begins with Ribera (1912) and ends with recent publications. The author's consideration of a polygenetic theory of origins is not — as it has been so often for others — an easy escape from decision; rather, it derives from careful thought and evaluation of the facts as known. A survey of the 562 compositions using the *zéjel* form (from the earliest to 1933) covers all of the Peninsula and treats equally of stylistic, thematic, and musical evolution. Significantly, no clear and direct link to Arabic poetry of this type can be established. The *CSM* are dealt with *passim* and especially on pp. 92-103 and 231-4, in the chapter on music, and in Appendix E (dealing with the unusually great number of unorthodox enjambements in Alfonso's poetry). Two observations are noteworthy and useful: that the refrain of the poem may not have been sung after each strophe in actual practice; and that some of the *cantigas* are basically mini-dramas and may well have been performed in some primitive dramatic form when sung (*CSM* 65 is used as illustration of this potential).

349   Mettmann, Walter, "Airas Nunes, Mitautor der *CSM*", *Ibero-romania*, III (1971), 8-10.

The rubric 'Airas Nunes' appears in the margin of *CSM* 223. M. presents reasons, based mostly on linguistic and stylistic comparisons of this *cantiga* with the known work of Nunes, supporting the belief that the

Galician poet was a contributor to the *CSM*. Discussion is brief, well-argued, and authoritative.

350   Scholberg, Kenneth R., *Sátira e invectiva en la España medieval* (Biblioteca Románica Hispánica, Estudios y Ensayos, 163, Madrid: Gredos, 1971), pp. 58-134.
Though references to Alfonso's satirical poetry are made throughout the volume, it is ch. II, "La sátira gallego-portuguesa en los siglos XIII y XIV", which helps to deepen our understanding of Alfonso's contributions to the panorama of the varied genres of satire and invective, both in his age and after it. Integrated into the purview given by S. are the following poems of Alfonso X: 23, 29, 7, 419, 427, 18, 14, 149, 12, 19, 31, 2, 16, 26, 21, 34, 10, and 3 (numbers are from Lapa [ed. of 1970], see entry for 1965).

1972

351   Ackerlind, Sheila Rogers, "The Relationship of Alfonso X of Castile to Diniz of Portugal", unpubl. diss., Yale Univ., 1972. 238 pp. An abstract appears in *DAI*, XXXIII (1972-3), 2358A.
The author shows, in one chapter, that the poems of Alfonso X provided inspiration and motivation to his grandson Dinis as well as a cultural background and a model for the latter's poetic court. However, there are few textual links. Other chapters go into Alfonso's influence in non-poetical ways.

352   Davis, William R., "Mary and Merlin: An Unusual Alliance", *RoN*, XIV (1972-3), 207-12.
An exploration of *CSM* 108 in which a prayer of Merlin's to Mary is answered. The article credits Alfonso with knowing at least fragments of the Arthurian legends then circulating, and especially the Grail story. D.'s discussion shows how reasonable the hypothesis is.

353   Keller, John E., "The Depiction of Exotic Animals in *Cantiga* XXIX of the *CSM*", in *Studies in Honor of Tatiana Fotitch* (Washington, D.C.: Catholic Univ. Press and Consortium Press, 1972), pp. 247-53.
The *Crónica de los reyes de Castilla* is witness to the arrival of all manner of exotic animals from Africa, most the gifts of Egypt's king. These denizens of Alfonso's zoo must have provided models for the animals depicted so clearly in the miniatures of *cantiga* 29.

354   Snow, Joseph T., "The *Loor* to the Virgin and its Appearance in the *CSM* of Alfonso el Sabio", unpubl. diss., Univ. of Wisconsin, 1972. 385 pp. An abstract appears in *DAI*, XXXII (1971-2), 5808A.

S. traces the poetic tradition in the West of the praise of Mary which reaches its high-water mark with the Alfonsine *loor*. The forty-two *loores* are treated on many fronts: rhyme schemes, musical schemes, imagistic unity, and literary merits. The study attempts to show how independent a creative artist Alfonso was in the *CSM* in general and in its lyric sections in particular.

355   Vandrey, Philip Lee, "A Stylistic Approach to the Author-ship Problem of the *CSM* of Alfonso el Sabio", unpubl. diss., Northwestern Univ., 1972. 113 pp. An abstract appears in *DAI*, XXXIII (1972-3), 5753A.
An exposition, through stylistic analysis, of the theory that Alfonso may well have been the sole author of the *CSM*. The main point V. makes is that a uniformity obtains throughout in terms of versification, rhyme, format, introductory formulas, and certain images. The ideas are interesting but, given the brevity of the study, far from conclusive. One alternative is that Alfonso exercised a strong editorial control over the compositions that were to be ultimately included. Still, this is a vital problem we must now face in further consideration of the art of the *CSM* and V. has started us off on the right foot.

1973

356   Bagby, Albert I., Jr, "The Moslem in the *Cantigas* of Alfonso X, el Sabio", *KRQ*, XX (1973), 173-207.
Tries to show — on the basis of 27 unfavourable presentations of the Muslim in a total of 42 *cantigas* where he is present — that Alfonso X is guilty of personal intolerance. This view is ingenuous and must be treated with some skepticism. B. notes that eight of the *CSM* treat the Muslim as virtuous, but he does not consider which of these conflicting representations indicate Alfonso's real feelings, which of the poems were written by Alfonso himself, or whether any of the literary roles created correspond to the poet's attitude rather than to a wish to create varied situations. The article is based on B.'s dissertation (1968).

357   *Cancioneiro português da Biblioteca Vaticana* (*Códice 4803*), introd. by Luís F. Lindley Cintra (Lisbon: Centro de Estudos Filológicos, 1973). xviii + 458 pp.
This makes available to the scholar for the first time a good facsimile ed. of *CV*; nineteen of the compositions belong to Alfonso X (nos 61-79).

358   Peña, Margarita, *Antología de Alfonso el Sabio* (Sepan Cuantos, 229, Mexico City: Ed. Porrúa, 1973).
Peña provides general comments (safe for a first introduction in schools),

and an adequate vocabulary, but uses Valmar's 1889 ed. instead of the more recent and reliable Mettmann (1959-72). From the *CSM* the inclusions are Prol. B, 4, 9, 56, 64, 94, 132, 142, 144, 180, 195, 279, 386, 401, and 406. From *CV* there are 75, 77, 79 and from *CB* 362, 363, 365, 368, and 370. The usefulness of all inclusions (and especially of the secular poems) is severely restricted by lack of notes.

359   Ramos, Epifanio, *Las cantigas de escarnio y maldecir de Alfonso X* (Lugo: Reprografía Alvarellos, 1973). 73 pp.
The title is promising but the book is disappointing. Only one *cantiga* is discussed at any length (Rodrigues Lapa 33) and a few others are briefly taken up (nos 10, 14, 17, 23, 11, and 7) but with no critical assessment. The study is fleshed out with rhetorical questions (see the chapter on Alfonso and his grandson Dinis of Portugal) which are maddeningly unproductive.

360   Sancho de Sopranís, Hipólito, *Mariología medieval xericiense*, ed. by M. Ruiz Lagos (Jerez de la Frontera: Centro de Estudios Históricos Jerezanos, 1973), pp. 9-15.
This section of the author's posthumously-issued notes relates the founding and building of the city of Santa María del Puerto by utilizing the *CSM* details recorded faithfully by Alfonso and his collaborators. The author's earlier works (see, for example, 1964) are better organized and more illuminating.

361   Walker, Roger M., "Two Notes on Spanish Debate Poems", in *Medieval Studies in Honor of Robert White Linker* (Madrid: Ed. Castalia, 1973), pp. 177-84.
Only the first of the two notes treats of Alfonso (pp. 177-80). In it, W. hints that Alfonso, in *CV* 64, may have indicated a knowledge of the text of the *Razón de amor*. This supposition hinges on the naming, in the *cantiga*, of two of the three European centres of courtly learning mentioned in the *Razón*. This seems rather slim support for the deductions that follow, although the ideas are original and provocative.

1974

362   Chisman, Anna Mary McGregor, "Enjambement in *Las* [sic] *Cantigas de Santa Maria* of Alfonso X, el Sabio", unpubl. diss., Univ. of Toronto, 1974. An abstract appears in *DAI*, XXXVI (1975-6), 1550-1A.
The closest scrutiny to date of Alfonso's unusual practices of enjambement, this study concludes that Alfonso is closer to Latin theories of composition than to either Provençal or Galician-Portuguese practice in his disruptive (often even violently so) displays of run-on lines.

In the narrative *miragres* enjambement speeds the pace of the story. Where there is no story line, as in the *loores*, enjambement is less striking. This implies that here Alfonso is less faithful to theory and more experimental in his own right: yet another way in which the *loores* show marked invention in contrast to the *miragres*.

362 bis   Cómez Ramos, Rafael, "La arquitectura en las miniaturas", in *Arquitectura alfonsí* (Seville: Diputación Provincial, 1974), pp. 103-34.
The volume is interesting throughout because of the generous use of black and white plates of the miniatures of the *CSM*. In the brief texts both civil and religious architecture are adequately commented upon: more eloquent, however, is the juxtaposition of miniatures with actual photographs to illustrate points the text is making. C.R. provides another sober reflection on Alfonsine illumination as a reliable presentation of the thirteenth-century world.

363   Davis, William R., "Another Aspect of the Virgin Mary in the *CSM*", *Revista de Estudios Hispánicos*, VIII (1974), 95-105.
A further aid to the scholar interested in the classification of the *CSM*. D. here focusses upon both the aggressive actions and the strong language used by the Virgin in *cantigas* 233, 63, 264, 47, 123, 11, 183, 61, 229, 283, 35, 286, 216, 42, 336, 274, and 32. These illustrations help him to show how human and temperamentally well-rounded was the Mediatrix between medieval man and his God.

364   Keller, John E., and Robert W. Linker, "Las traducciones castellanas de las *CSM*", *BRAE*, LIV (1974), 221-93.
As the authors admit, these are not really translations (an exception is later found in the prose of *cantiga* 10), but rather a kind of exposition – using more ample texts as a basis – of the content of *CSM* 2-25. The Spanish prose is penned in the margin of Escurial MS T.j.l.
• This article gives an edition of the texts (see Chatham [1976]) and discusses one, *CSM* 11, at length. Two opinions offered us in the introduction are open to question: that Alfonso commissioned these Castilian summaries (p. 223), and that the aim was to make the contents more understandable to "ciertas capas de la sociedad española del siglo XIII" (p. 222).

365   Keller, John E., and Charles L. Nelson, "Some Remarks on Visualization in the *CSM*", *Ariel* (una publicación de los estudiantes graduados del Departamento de Español e Italiano de la Univ. de Kentucky), III, no. 1 (abril, 1974), 7-12.
A description of the way in which the artist or artists of *CSM* 22

follow the verse narration. Curiously, the artist depicts a scene of worship in his final panel, whereas the poetic text never gets that far. One may find then that in the case of well-known miracles the artists were influenced by what they already knew and were not always restricted by the Alfonsine text.

366   López Serrano, Matilde, *Cantigas de Santa Maria de Alfonso X el Sabio, rey de Castilla* (Madrid: Patrimonio Nacional, 1974). 74 pp.
This pleasant survey of the *CSM*'s art, music and MSS makes no claim to originality. There are 16 full-colour miniatures from *cantigas* 1, 2, 8, 10, 23, 42, 63, 94, 107, 108, 133, 142, 165, 167, 172, and 187, and *CSM* 144 appears on the dustjacket. The quality and clarity of these vary from acceptable to somewhat blurred. A few curiosities crop up: L.S. believes that Alfonso knew Arabic perfectly (p. 9); she says that Escurial MS T.j.1 has 200 poems (there are 193); and she repeats the long-discredited view that the musical notation is rabbinical (p. 13). More care should have been taken in both text and clarity of reproductions.

367   Marsan, Rameline E., *Itinéraire espagnol du conte médiéval (VIIIe-XVe siècles).* (Témoins de l'Espagne, Série Historique, Paris: Klincksieck, 1974). 695 pp.
A sweeping study of no small interest to Alfonsine scholars, which covers many of the *CSM* and demonstrates how much in the mainstream of medieval narrative they were. These poems are listed in the detailed summary on pp. 667-95 but not all, unhappily, appear in the index (I found at least thirteen references to Alfonso unindexed, at least three of which include studies of *cantigas*: pp. 268, 290, and 428). M.'s commentary is useful, especially as her focus is comparative, thus making it one of the best broad studies of *CSM* analogues to date. *Cantigas* included deal with: mutilations, 174, 127, and *146* (pp. 231-2); suicide, *26* (p. 258); variations of the tale of the errant nun, *59*, 58, *55*, 94, and *285* (pp. 260-9); the contesting powers of heaven and hell, 3, 155, 281, *216* (pp. 283-91); the penitent man, *63* (pp. 301-2); profanations, 34, 215, 12, 128, 208, and 104 (pp. 303-15); the lower passions, 5 and *355* (pp. 418-25); cupidity, 175, 239, and *147* (pp. 428-9, 455); and infant deaths, 4, 6, and 17 (pp. 547-50). The *CSM* in italics are those which appear, in full, in the Appendix.
One note of caution. References to miracles and shrines given on pp. 159-61 and in the corresponding notes on pp. 184-5 are faulty. For note 51, *CSM* 127 and 148 should be replaced by 302 and 311. In note 54, *CSM* 227, 234, and 243 are omitted. In note 56, *CSM* 227 and 293 are wrongly placed while the more appropriate 228 and

283 are omitted. In note 57, *CSM* 118 is left out. In note 58 (on Tudía) *CSM* 344 ought to be included.
The bibliography, given the scope of the work, is very ample.

368   Montoya Martínez, Jesús, "Criterio agrupador de las *CSM*", in *Estudios literarios dedicados al profesor Mariano Baquero Goyanes* (Murcia, 1974), pp. 285-96.
This classification scheme is built upon a system suggested by the *cantigas* and not by an external system such as thematic grouping. The author suggests an allegorical view of the roles of the Virgin (as protector, as medicine, as refuge, etc.) as a better way to deal with the variety of the *cantigas* than was Valmar's system of rather arbitrary divisions. While this study is too brief to do proper justice to such a broad theme, it should send us to the author's Univ. of Murcia thesis (which I have not yet seen), which develops it at length. Model *cantigas* for some of the author's intriguing plan are *CSM* 57, 17, 13, 23, and 386. This study has the virtue of injecting truly new blood into the search for a satisfactory way to classify the *CSM*, and reveals more of the inner workings of the collection than classification heretofore.

369   Pensado, José L., "En torno a una cantiga de escarnio del Rey Sabio", *Verba*, I (1974), 41-53.
An essay in comparative philology which, by discussing Romance offshoots of Latin 'vetus', 'vetere', and 'vetulu', is aimed at clarifying the expression 'espargendo vedo' of *CBN* 441. P.'s resolution of the phrase's meaning is the most satisfactory thus far for the specific context.

1975

369 bis   Álvarez Blázquez, J.M., *Escolma da poesía medieval: 1198-1354* (Col. Pombal, Série Poética, XV, Vigo: Ed. Castrelos, 1975), pp. 62-73.
This volume, entirely in Galician, is different from its 1952 forerunner in that there are three new poets and 30 new poems plus corrected and expanded biographical notes where appropriate. The glossary covers most of the more unusual words and the 8-page bibliography, while not complete, lists items as recent as 1974. The selection of Alfonsine texts remains unchanged: *CSM* 10, 103, 260, 351, 406 and *CV* 63, 73, and 79.

370   Chisman, Anna McGregor, "The Symbolism of Diseases in the *CSM* of Alfonso X" (abstract), in *La Corónica*, III, no. 2 (Spring 1975), 3.
C.'s basic idea is that disease is used as a punishment for sin in the *CSM*.

This seems borne out by identities and parallels in both the conceptual and linguistic realization for the 75 poems which treat of disease and illness. The complete form of this item is, as yet, unpublished.

371   Keller, John E., "A Feasible Source of the Denouements of the *Exemplos* in *El Conde Lucanor*", *American Notes & Queries*, XIV, no. 3 (Nov. 1975), 34-7.
K. advances the thought that the format of the prose versions of the early *cantigas* (2-25) of the Escurial MS J.b.2 of the *CSM* could have been a model for Don Juan Manuel's arrangement of the materials in the individual tales in *El Conde Lucanor*. K. too easily accepts that Alfonso is responsible for these prose accounts but, even so, he points out enough parallels to warrant further study of this possible literary contact between uncle and nephew.

372   ——, "An Unknown Castilian Lyric Poem: The Alfonsine Translation of *Cantiga* X of the *CSM*", *HR*, XLIII (1975), 43-7.
K. shows that a generally faithful Castilian verse rendering of *cantiga* 10 lies concealed among the prose summaries of the first 25 *cantigas* (see Keller and Linker [1974]). A possible reason (not suggested by K.) for this solitary verse rendering is that, while prose accounts of miracles were available as precedents for the summaries of the other *cantigas*, this was not the case with this lyric of praise.

373   Longland, Jean R., "A Preliminary Bibliography of Medieval Galician-Portuguese Poetry in English Translation", in *Studies in Honor of Lloyd A. Kasten* (Madison, Wisconsin: Hispanic Seminary of Medieval Studies, 1975), pp. 135-53.
On pp. 138-9 there is a listing of English versions of: *CSM* Prol. B, 5, 7, 10, 11, 18, 40, 79, 84, 94, 144, 169, 228, and 406; *CBN* 398 and 411; and *CV* 63, 64, 69, 75, and 76. These include both complete and partial translations, in verse and in prose.

374   Snow, Joseph T., "Alfonso X y la *Cantiga* 409: Un nexo posible con la tradición de la *Danza de la Muerte*", in *Studies in Honor of Lloyd A. Kasten* (Madison, Wisconsin: Hispanic Seminary of Medieval Studies, 1975), pp. 261-73.
Rather than attempt a direct link between the poems, S. investigates the specific combination of literary motifs which give shape and structure to the poems discussed. He shows that Alfonso has written a *danza de la muerte* characterized by joy, not gloom. He does so by accounting for the social and intellectual distance between the periods

of composition of the two poems and concludes that both are manifestations of a single poetic genre, or sub-genre, of the medieval literature of death.

1976

375 Chatham, James R., "A Paleographic Edition of the Alfonsine Collection of Prose Miracles of the Virgin", in *Oelschläger Festschrift* (Estudios de *Hispanófila*, XXXVI, Chapel Hill, 1976), pp. 73-111.

C. presents a full and respectable paleographic transcription of the Castilian prose summaries of *CSM* 2-25, and provides valuable prefatory material which reviews the wide range of potential sources for these particular *cantigas*. C. finds the Keller-Linker article (1974) incomplete and sometimes inaccurate. He concludes that it is extremely difficult to determine the way in which the legends found their home in the *CSM*, but he appends to each prose account notes on the locations of medieval texts and analogues to it. These Alfonsine prose miracles are rarely translations of the verse text; they even add material not directly accounted for in it. An even more suggestive note is encountered in the biographical reference to Alfonso in the prose accompanying *cantiga* 10. A very worthwhile study which will surely be the basis for future work on these prose miracles.

375 bis Domínguez Rodríguez, A., "Imágenes de presentación de la miniatura alfonsí", *Goya*, no. 131 (marzo-abril, 1976), pp. 287-91.

This is a sample of a longer study the author says he is preparing. It focusses on the large miniatures at the beginning (usually) of a MS in which is depicted a scene of the king-as-patron receiving a finished copy of the work he had commissioned. Alfonsine MSS were truly the first to include such scenes as a regular feature. The *CSM* illumination has a secular artistic style and is obviously very carefully supervised by Alfonso as well as highly valued. The presentation scenes from the two Escurial MSS are reproduced and the larger of the two from MS T.j.l appears on the cover, in colour. The commentary concentrates on traits of style common to these scenes in several Alfonsine texts.

376 Keller, John E., "Verbalization and Visualization in the *CSM*", in *Oelschläger Festschrift* (Estudios de *Hispanófila*, XXXVI, Chapel Hill, 1976), pp. 221-6.

Describes the six miniatures illustrating Alfonso's version of the Theophilus legend (*CSM* 3) and explores the correlation of these visual guides to the account given in the poem. K. explains the pictorial details not specifically mentioned in the text as having derived, perhaps, from familiar accounts of greater length. This study is one part of a project of Keller's which promises further investigation of the relationship of the poetic texts to their pictorial realization. Further steps will be necessary to determine which of the available accounts might have been utilized as a basis for the miniatures.

ADDENDA

1854

24
bis
Schack, Adolph Friedrich von, *Geschichte der dramatischen Literatur und Kunst in Spanien* (Frankfurt-am-Main: Joseph Baer, 1854). The Spanish translation, by Eduardo de Mier, Madrid: M. Tello, 5 vols, 1885-8, with relevant sections in vol. I, pp. 194-8 and 217-19.
with relevant sections in vol. I, pp. 194-8 and 217-19.
Pages 194-8 (Spanish version) contain an early summary of the main points of the poetic letter and reply (*Supplicatio* and *Declaratio*) exchanged between Guiraut Riquier and Alfonso X, in which Alfonso's position as arbiter in matters of poetry is made evident (for good modern editions of these, and commentary, see Bertolucci Pizzorusso [1966] and Vuolo [1968]). The appreciation of the *CSM* on pp. 217-19 is of no scholarly value; however, it takes note of, and credits Alfonso with, a strong effort to revive the waning troubadour fashion in lyric poetry.

1856

25
bis
Morayta de Sagrario, Miguel, "Las *Cantigas* de Don Alonso el Sabio", *La Discusión*, Diario democrático (Madrid), no. 175 (25 sept., 1856), pp. 1-2; no. 178 (28 sept., 1856), pp. 1-2; no. 183 (4 oct., 1856), pp. 1-2; no. 189 (11 oct., 1856), pp. 1-2.
These articles set out to revalue Alfonso's worth as a "guerrero, legislador y poeta" but succeed only in the latter. M. rejects, along with Amador, the attribution of the *Querellas* to Alfonso. With the *CSM*, his greatest work, Alfonso is credited with extending devotion to the Virgin, a devotion that also took the form of the establishment of a short-lived Military Order. M. thinks Alfonso alone wrote the words and music for the *CSM* but cannot satisfactorily explain the choice of Galician as a poetic medium. He dates them, from internal evidence, between 1263 and 1279 (both of which dates now seem conservative). He praises the excellence of the *loores* (esp. *cantigas* 110, 150, 140, 340, 10, and 70) and the variety of the *milagros*. He believes that *CSM*

113

32 has made use of Berceo's poem on the same theme. The concluding section stresses the dramatic content of several of the narrative poems, especially *cantigas* 105, 42, 16, 84, and 347. Although sketches rather than studies, these articles are the first to seriously assess the literary worth of the *CSM* (see also M.'s publication of selected texts, 1862).

1866

31   Rioja, A.P., "Revista teatral", in *La Reforma* (Madrid),
bis   (4 marzo, 1866), p. 3; (11 marzo, 1866), p. 1.
In the section headed "Folletín de *La Reforma*", of both dates, is a review of the third in a series of sacred music presentations at the Teatro Real (which took place on Friday, March 2). High praise is given to the fourth song in the program's third section, "Cantiga XIV del Rey D. Alfonso el Sabio, [cantada] por la señorita Velasco, acompañándola el cuerpo de coros de este coliseo, y el de niños alumnos del Conservatorio, parafraseada por el maestro Eslaba" (see Eslava [1865]).

1870

31   Varnhagen, F.A., *Cancioneirinho de trovas antigas colligidas*
tris   *de um grande cancioneiro da Bibliotheca do Vaticano*
(Vienna: Typographia I.E.R. do E.E. da Corte, 1870). 34 + 170 pp. (throughout the latter continuous pagination, texts appear in roman and notes in arabic numerals).
Interested by Wolf's description (1859) of these newly uncovered poems, V. had a transcription made of a Madrid copy and checked it against MS Vatican 4803. The 34 pages of "notícia crítica" never had much critical value: however, they reveal the story of how a selection of *CV* first found its way into print (better and more reliable editions were soon to follow; see Monaci [1875] and Braga [1878]). V. states there are 21 Alfonsine compositions but has miscounted: there are 19 plus one shared *tenson*. The two *cantigas profanas* of Alfonso made available (pp. cxxx-cxxxiv) are *CV* 79 and 77 (in his edition, numbers XLVIII and XLIX).

1881

40   Aznar y García, Francisco, *Indumentaria española: docu-*
bis   *mentos para su estudio*, 2nd ed. (Madrid, 1881), unpaginated.
There is no text, only a series of 288 *estampas*, all drawn by Aznar. The four that are based on the *CSM* come from Escurial MS J.b.2, depicting variously-garbed musicians. These carry numbers XXXIX, LXXIV,

LXXV, and LXXXVII. In addition there are others, some similar, from the Alfonsine work, *Libro de las tablas.*

1905

71
bis

Pérez de Guzmán, Juan, "La biblioteca de consulta de D. Alfonso el Sabio", *La Ilustración Española y Americana,* LXXIX (1905), 131-4.

This is a useful first step but more work along these lines could be done. Two documents are reproduced which attest to Alfonso's borrowing of books for use in his scriptorium. P. de G. estimates Alfonso may have had as many as 150 vols and took great pride in producing the books that he was lacking, and in the creation of new works. Attributed to Alfonso are the *Querellas,* the *Libro del tesoro,* the *Cantigas* and the mysteriously-titled *Decires* (the *cantigas profanas?*).

1925

121
bis

Filgueira Valverde, José, "San Ero d'Armenteira", *Nós,* no. 22 (1925), [pp. 3-4].

This item was not seen but very likely is a continuation of the item F.V. published in the issue of *Nós* immediately preceding (see 1925).

APPENDIX A: Editions of the *cantigas profanas*

Not all studies of Alfonso's poetry have had recourse to the same MSS or editions and their numbering varies more often than not. For the *CSM* Mettmann has solved this problem in a table (1959, vol. I) which summarizes the contents of all four of the manuscripts, and his numbering must now be considered definitive for all future study. The present appendix attempts to organize the various editions of the *cantigas profanas* of Alfonso: all of these are represented in col. 1 whose numbering is that of the MS once owned by Colocci and indexed by Brancuti, which is now in Lisbon's Biblioteca Nacional. It is most often referred to as Colocci-Brancuti but I have used *MS* to designate it. One modern edition of this MS exists (see *infra*, Machado, 1949) and the position of the Alfonsine compositions in this edition is noted in col. 2, under the rubric *CBN* (*Cancioneiro da Biblioteca Nacional*).

Some of these poems appear also in Vatican MS 4803, known most commonly as the *Cancioneiro da Vaticana*, which was edited twice in the last century (by Monaci in 1875 and by Braga in 1878, see *infra*). We now possess a facsimile of *CV*, issued in 1973 by the Centro de Estudos Filológicos, with a preface by L.F. Lindley Cintra. The numbers of Alfonso's poems from this work appear in col. 3. In col. 4 appear the numbers assigned to Alfonso's compositions which appeared in Molteni's ed. of the Colocci-Brancuti MS (1880); these differ from other editions because Molteni did not choose to include those already published from *CV* by Monaci. Here, the col. heading is *CB*.

In 1965 M. Rodrigues Lapa gave us his edition of the *cantigas d'escarnho e de mal dizer* which he gathered from all the *cancioneiros*. These are finely edited and carry his own numbers, which appear in col. 5. Finally, when Tavani published his monumental *Repertorio metrico della lirica galego-portoghese* (1967), he united much useful information on all 46 poems. Although he did not edit them anew I have included his numbers in col. 6 (from pp. 386-90 of the book) because of the importance of this contribution to the study of Alfonsine poetry. For quick recognition, I have also given the *incipit*, when possible, from Lapa's ed. and, failing this, from that of the Machados.

Incipit	1 MS	2 *CBN*	3 *CV*	4 *CB*	5 Lapa	6 Tavani
Ay eu coitada	456	398		348		18.2
Mester avia Don·Gil	457	399		349	27	18.25
Achei Sancha Anes enca- valgada	458	400		350	28	18.1
Penhoremos o daian	459	401		351	29	18.32
Med'ei ao pertigueiro	460	402		352	30	18.24
Direi-vos eu d'un Ricomen	461	403		353	31	18.10
Tanto sei de vos, ricomen	462	404		354	32	18.43
Se me graça fezesse este Papa de Roma	463	405		355	33	18.39
Dom Rodrigo moordomo	464	406		356	34	18.17
Hũa pregunt'ar quer a el Rei fazer	465[1]	407		357	149	18.44
Don Gonçalo, pois queredes ir daqui	466	408		358	35	18.14
Deus te salue, gloriosa	467[2]	409		359		18.9
Falar quer eu da senhor ben cousida	468	410		360		18.18
Ben sabia eu, mha senhor	468[3]	411		360[3]		18.5
Pois que m'ei ora d'alongar	469	412		361		18.36
Par Deus Senhor	470	413		362		18.31
Senhora, por amor Deus	471[4]	414		363		18.40
[Maria Pérez vi muit' assanhada]	-----[5]	415		364	1	18.23
Pero que ei ora mengua de companha	472	416		365	2	18.35
Don Ayras, pois me rogades	473	417		366	3	18.12
Don Meendo, vos veestes	474	418		367	4	18.16
Don Meendo, Don Meendo	474[6]	419		368	6	18.15
Falauan duas irmanas	475	420		369	5	18.19
Non quer'eu donzela fea	476	421		370	7	18.27
Senher, ara ie·us vein quer[er]	477[7]	422		371	427	18.42

Appendix A: Editions of the cantigas profanas

Incipit	1 MS	2 CBN	3 CV	4 CB	5 Lapa	6 Tavani
. . . e com[e] omen que quer mal doitear	478	423	61	372	8	18.22
Vi un coteife muy granhon	479	424	62		9	18.46
Non me posso pagar tanto	480	425	63		10	18.26
Joan Rodriguez foi esmar a Balteira	481	426	64		11	18.21
Ansur Moniz, muit'ouve gran pesar	482	427	65		12	18.3
Senhor, iustiça vimos pedir	483	428	66		13	18.41
Fui eu poer a mão	484	429	67		14	18.20
Pero da Pont'á feito gran pecado	485	430	68		15	18.33
Don Foan, de quand'ogano i chegou	486	431	69		16	18.13
Pero da Ponte, parou-se-vos mal	487	432	70		17	18.34
Cítola, oi andar-se queixando	488	433	71		18	18.6
Quero-vos ora mui ben conselhar	489	434	72		19	18.37
Com'eu en dia de Pascoa	490	435	73		20	18.7
O genete/pois remete	491	436	74		21	18.28
De grado queria ora saber	492	437	75		22	18.8
Ao daian de Cález eu achei	493	438	76		23	18.4
O que foy passar a serra	494	439	77		24	18.30
Domingas Eanes ouve sa batalha	495	440	78		25	18.11
O que da guerra levou cavaleiros	496	441	79		26	18.29
Rei D. Alfonso, se Deus vos perdon	1512[8]	1424		385	419	18.38
Ũa pregunta vos quero fazer	1624[9]	1528	1158		303	18.45

[1] A tenson with Garcia Pérez.

[2] Also in CSM, no. 40, a loor of the Virgin.

[3] This composition was considered joined to the fragment preceding it although there are two spaces in the MS separating them.

[4] This fragment is Alfonso's only known poetic text in Castilian.

5 There is no separate number for this poem as it is treated as part of the Castilian poem preceding.

6 The MS repeats the same number as for the preceding composition though they are two different texts.

7 A *tenson* with Arnaldo (Arnaut Catalan?).

8 A *tenson* with Vaasco Gil.

9 A *tenson* with Paai Gomez Charinho.

APPENDIX B: Citations of Alfonso's Poems

This Appendix forms an index to the *cantigas* of Alfonso X mentioned in the titles and annotations of this bibliography. The numbers for the *CSM* correspond to their position in Mettmann's ed. (1959-64). Those for the *cantigas profanas* refer to the Machado ed. of the *CBN* (1949-64) since all of the secular poems are included and each has a distinct number. A potential — if unavoidable — problem arises here in that I have thought it best to retain the numbering of the different editions used by authors in my annotations of their contributions. This can be easily resolved, however, by quick consultation of Appendix A where all numbering systems are collated. Italic numbers indicate a text without commentary, e.g. in an anthology.

1. The *Cantigas de Santa Maria*

In addition to the listing given below, I ought to mention that several items in the bibliography treat of the *CSM* more generally and I have found that listing the *cantigas* treated would have been unproductive: in some cases, it would have called for listing all of them. Instead, I shall mention here the numbers of these items in one list for constant reference. These items are: 49, 65, 67, 111, 119, 132, 135, 151, 185, 220, 224, 266, *275*, *301*, 302, 319, 329, 344, 348, 355, 356, and 362.

Prologue A: 9, 14, 297

Prologue B: 7, 14, 21, *109*, *126*, *162*, 315, 320, *358*, 373

1:106, 113, *126*, 129, *150*, 212, 221, *245*, 256, *294*, 335, 354, 366

2: 14, 25, 41, *73*, 117, 124, *150*, 170, 187, 212, 254, 256, 257, 345, 347, 364, 366, 375

3: 34, 41, 212, 347, 364, 367, 375, 376

4: 41, 62, *109*, 124, 154, 199, *203*, 212, 214, 254, 298, *343*, 345, 347, *358*, 364, 367, 375

5: *150*, 154, 177, 178, 212, 338, 345, 364, 367, 373, 375

6: 25, 124, 154, 212, 214, 330, 345, 347, 364, 367, 375

7: 124, 154, 178, 212, 364, 373, 375

8: 74, 124, *150*, 154, 212, *258*, 364, 366, 375

9: *109*, 124, *150*, 187, 212, 256, *358*, 364, 375

10: 25 bis, 63, 72, 79, 83, 85, *126*, 149, *150*, *162*, 170, 172, 181, 183, 198, 211, 212, *228*, *237*, *244*, 252, *294*, 305, 320, 324, 337, 354, 364, 366, *369 bis*, 372, 373, 375

11: 41, 42, 124, 154, 184, 212, 363, 364, 373, 375

12: 41, 124, 158, 212, 256, 345, 347, 364, 367, 375

13: 41, 124, 154, 212, 364, 368, 375

14: 31, 31 bis, 41, 124, 154, 212, 346, 364, 375

15: 41, 124, 154, 212, 239, 254, 364, 375

16: 25 bis, *29*, 124, *150*, 154, 304, 364, 375

17: 25, 83, 124, 154, 178, 364, 367, 368, 375

18: 212, 246, 272, 364, 373, 375

19: 41, 124, 212, 269, 364, 375

20: *126*, *150*, 212, 268, 354, 364, 375

21: 41, 55, 124, 212, 320, 364, 375

22: 212, 235, 347, 364, 365, 375

23: 41, 47, 124, 212, 364, 366, 368, 375

24: 41, 124, *150*, 154, 170, 212, 256, 280, 330, 364, 375

25: 41, 124, 135, 154, 212, 335, 345, 347, 364, 375

26: 41, 124, 154, 178, 187, 235, 320, 367

27: 41, 124, 212, 345, 347

28: 25, 71, 96, 124, 146, 154, 170, 212, 256, 312, 335, 339

29: 41, 124, 212, 315, 353

30: 106, *126*, 268, 354

31: 304

32: 25 bis, 41, 72, 124, 154, 256, 363

33: 41, 124, 154, 212, 335

34: 41, 72, 124, 154, 304, 345, 347, 367

35: 124, 154, 212, 256, 335, 363

36: 41, 42, 124, *150*, 154, *258*

37: 41, 124, 154

38: 34, 79, 124

39: 41, 83, 124, 212, 300

40: 59, 79, 212, 215, 268, 296, 354, 373

41: 83, 124, 212

42: 25 bis, *29*, 42, 154, 157, 212, 272, 274, 279, 346, 363, 366

43: 91

44: 80, 91, 212, 256

45: 41, 124, 154, 212

46: 124, 154, 256, 257

47: 41, 82, 124, 154, 170, 298, 363

48: 116, 212, 216, 288

49: 41, 124, 323

50: 82, 126, 129, 354

51: 41, 124, 154, 212, 347

52: 83, 86, 116, 144, 171, 212, 216, 288

53: 41, 124, 154

54: 34, 41, 124, 135, 154, 212, 214

55: 34, 68, 131, 178, 367

56: 86, *109*, 124, *150*, 154, 212, 214, 229, 304, 335, *358*

57: 83, 116, 170, 187, 212, 216, 240, 254, 288, 368

58: 68, 86, 124, 154, 178, 212, 367

59: 68, 178, 212, 250, 256, 367

60: 55, 71, 82, 96, *109*, *126*, 212, 266, 312, 313, 315, 324, 341, 354

61: 41, 71, 102, 124, 154, 312, 363

62: 41, 124, 149

63: 29, 41, 56, 68, 124, 177, 335, 363, 366, 367

64: *29*, *109*, 178, 190, 212, 256, *358*

65: 71, 102, 124, 154, 312, 316, 320, 348

66: 41, 124, 154, 257

67: 34, 41, 124, 154, 212

68: 106, 154, 178, 212, 254

69: 50, 83, 320

70: 25 bis, 55, 85, *126*, *150*, *258*, *294*, 324, 354

71: 82, 124, 154, 347

72: 34, 124, 304, 330

73: 41, 124

74: 124, 256, 272, 315

75: 124, 330

76: 113, 124, 212

77: 72, 198, 212, 235

78: *73*, 212, 266

79: 51, 124, 298, 373

80: *126*, 354

81: 41, 124, 154

82: - -

83: 212

84: 25 bis, 34, 124, *150*, 373

85: 124, 345, 347

86: 41, 124, 212

87: 41, 42, 124, 135, 256

88: 124

89: 124, 345, 347

90: 82, 260, 354

91: 194, 221, 347

92: - -

93: 113, 194, 212, 221, 266

94: 32, 68, *109*, 124, 131, *150*, 178, 194, 221, 229, 235, 256, 304, *358*, 366, 367, 373

95: 177, 194, 346

96: 212

97: 266

98: 178, 194, 221, 304

99: 256

100: 72, 79, 129, 324, 354

101: 41, 48, 124

102: - -

103: 34, *73*, 101, 121, 125, *150*, 164, 229, *237*, 256, *258*, *264*, *369 bis*

104: 34, 178, 235, 346, 367

105: 25 bis, 124, 154, 328

106: 41, 124

107: 43, *162*, 174, 178, 246, 256, 257, 269, 272, 315, 345, 347, 366

108: 256, 266, 332, 335, 345, 347, 352, 366

109: 91, 345

110: 25 bis, 194, 200, 354

111: 41, 42, 254

112: 266

113: 116, 212, 216, 288

114: 91

115: 55, 82, 94, 124, 154, 178, 187, 266

116: - -

117: 194, 212

118: 91, 106, 194, 367

119: 72, 79

120: 113, 354

121: - -

122: 34, 328

123: 212, 363

124: 72, 79, 106, 250, 256

125: 41, 42, 124, 178

126: 83, 199, 212, 256

127: 212, 367

128: 34, 124, *150*, 246, 254, 346, 367

129: 91, 266

130: 98, 256, 324, 354

131: 124

132: 3, 41, 42, *109*, 124, 154, 254, *358*

133: 83, 316, 347, 366

134: 194, 221, 254, 266, 316

135: 34, 347

136: 113, 212, 330

137: 194, 256

138: 254, 256, 266

139: 41, 79, 83, 124, 146, 250

140: 25 bis, 85, *126*, 354

141: 34, 194, 246, 254, 266

142: 80, *109*, 194, 256, 330, *358*, 366

143: 83, 256

144: *109*, 256, 335, *358*, 366, 373

145: 149, 254

146: 367

147: 74, 254, 367

148: 34, 82, 367

149: 82, 345, 346, 347

150: 25 bis, 83, 266, 354

151: 178

152: - -

153: 34, 74, 254

154: 124, 153, *244*, 256

155: 34, *150*

156: *150*, 346

157: 74, 254, 266, 315

158: 74, 254, 256

159: 74, 170, 254

160: 320, 354

161: 91, 266

162: 34, 266

163: 86, 91

164: 91, 268 bis

165: 149, 200, 292, 366

166: 91, 250

167: 91, 366

168: 91, 104, 268 bis

169: 82, 200, 214, 233, 256, 297, 315, 320, 373

170: 354

171: 91, 266

172: 91, 113, 366

173: 91, 268 bis

174: 106, 330, 367

175: 124, 207, 254, 256, 346, 367

176: 79, 266

177: 266

178: 333

179: 170, 199

180: *109*, 233, 266, 268, 324, 354, *358*

181: 177

182: 82, 266

183: 210, 266, 297, 335, 363

184: 106

185: 2, 178, 292, 339

186: 79, 339

187: 235, 266, 347, 366

188: 34

189: 79, 91

190: 354

191: --

192: --

193: 268 bis

194: 113

195: *109*, 124, 178, *358*

196: 34, 266

197: 230

198: 230

199: 230

200: 71, 102, *126*, *150*, 354

201: 178, 304

202: 278

203: 266

204: --

205: 177, 333

206: 124, *150*, 266, 304

207: 250

208: 34, 345, 346, 367

209: 97, 170, 233, 253

210: 82, *126*, 266, 354

211: 83, *150*, 194

212: 247, 266

213: 178

214: 74, 204

215: 34, 297, 339, 367

216: 41, 68, 124, 363, 367

217: --

218: 82, 273, 346

219: --

220: 82, 324, 354

221: 3, 4, 25, 34, 92, 96, 146, 297

222: 230

223: 57, 70, 230, 349

224: 230

225: --

226: --

227: 300, 367

228: 98 (*F* 88), 103 (*F* 88), 230, 256, 367, 373

229: 363

230: 71, 102, 354

231: 72, 124

232: 80

233: 363

234: 367

235: 297

236: --

237: 178, 230, 270

238: 34, 230, 330, 347

239: 266, 367

240: 266, 354

241: 82, 246

242: 80, 106

243: 330, 367

244: - -

245: 230, 270

246: 82, 97, 266

247: 91

248: - -

249: - -

250: *126*, *150*, 209, 354

251: 82

252: - -

253: 273

254: 41, 124, 266, 298

255: 34, 41, 124, 154, 198

256: 3, 4, 25, *73*, 96, *162*

257: 3

258: 199, 246

259: 83, 194

260: 82, *126*, *150*, 198, 209, *237*, 252, 324, 354, *369 bis*

261: 82

262: - -

263: - -

264: 82, 337, 345, 363

265: 124

266: - -

267: 270

268: - -

269: 124

270: 79, 82, 354

271: - -

272: 178

273: - -

274: 57, 363

275: 230

276: - -

277: 230

278: 98 (*F* 74), 103 (*F* 74), 273

279: 83, *109*, 144, 158, 233, 298, *358*

280: 354

281: 124, 367

282: 55

283: 34, 230, 266, 363, 367

284: 82

285: 68, 124, 131, 154, 178, 367

286: 304, 345, 347, 363

287: - -

288: 47, 48

289: 298

290: 83, *126*, 324, 354

291: - -

292: 3, 103 (*F* 10), 170

293: 82, 367

294: 266, 330

295: - -

296: 82

297: - -

298: 41, 124, 194, 268 bis

299: - -

300: *126*, 297, 354

301: 266, 268 bis
302: 116, 212, 216, 268 bis, 288, 367
303: 170
304: 235, 268 bis
305: 178, 345
306: 199
307: - -
308: 41, 124
309: 46, 123
310: 354
311: 116, 216, 288, 367
312: 34, 178, 190, 345, 347
313: - -
314: - -
315: 82, 272
316: *150*, 230
317: 268 bis, 298
318: 230
319: 230
320: 82, *126*, 260, 268, 354
321: - -
322: 106, *150*, 230
323: 3, 21, 297
324: 3, 10
325: 297, 298, 304
326: 268 bis
327: 199, 230, 330
328: 159 bis, 191 bis, 291, 297, 303
329: - -
330: 208, 324, 354
331: - -
332: - -
333: 230, 268 bis, 270

334: 230
335: *150*
336: - -
337: - -
338: 230
339: 83, 266, 320
340: 25 bis, 59, 79, *126*, *150*, 266 287, 354
341: - -
342: 230
343: 74
344: 367
345: 57, 303
346: - -
347: 25 bis, 169, 216
348: 337, 347
349: - -
350: *126*, 324, 354
351: *150*, *237*, 333, *369 bis*
352: 80, 235, 330
353: *150*, 170, 271
354: 199, 297, 333
355: 367
356: 291
357: 291, 304
358: 159 bis, 191 bis, 291
359: 291
360: 354
361: 169
362: 124, 154, 268 bis
363: - -
364: 159 bis, 191 bis, 291
365: - -

366: 80, 268 bis, 291, 297

367: 83, 159 bis, 191 bis, 266, 291

368: 82, 291

369: *150*, 177, 230

370: 194, 354

371: 191 bis, 291

372: 82, *150*, 291

373: *150*

374: 303

375: 268 bis, 284, 291

376: 291, 297

377: 284, 291, 297

378: 291

379: 82, 291, 339

380: 82, 354

381: 291

382: 284, 291

383: 191 bis

384: 124

385: 291

386: 268 bis, 297, *358*, 368

387: - -

388: - -

389: 291

390: 347, 354

391: 106, 291

392: 291

393: 268 bis, 291

394: - -

395: - -

396: *109*

397: - -

398: 191 bis, 291

399: 178, 230, 270

400: 354

401: 82, *109*, *126*, 233, 266, 377, *358*

402: 124, *126*

403: 221, 266

404: - -

405: 254, 266

406: 32, 59, *109*, *126*, *150*, 199, 209, 229, *237*, *244*, 260, *294*, 297, 313, 315, 341, *358*, *369 bis*, 373

407: 266

408: 46, 97

409: 97, 103, 268, 354, 374

410: 14, 83

411: 14, 82, 129

412: 266

413: 100, 129

414: - -

415: 266, 345, 347

416: 266

417: 129

418: 129

419: 82, 129, 225, 322, 345, 347

420: 82, 177, 266, 322

421: 266

422: 129

423: - -

424: 129

425: 129, 144, 171, 176, 266, 347

426: 129, 345, 346

427: 129

2. The *cantigas profanas*

Numbers in which many texts appear but for which I have not made a detailed listing include *37, 39, 40,* 222, 307, 318, and *357.*

CBN		*CBN*	
398:	161, *244,* 315, 373	423:	259
399:	- -	424:	- -
400:	331	425:	57, 64, 72, *237,* 259, 314, 321, 350, 359, *369 bis,* 373
401:	14, 311, 350		
402:	- -	426:	57, 58, 113, 311, 315, 359, 361, 373
403:	57, 350		
404:	- -	427:	336, 350
405:	359	428:	311
406:	350	429:	311, 350, 359
407:	350	430:	113, 120, 252, *264,* 277, 317
408:	57	431:	57, *264,* 315, 350, 373
409:	40, 215, 296, 315	432:	110, 113, 120, 208, 252, *264,* 277, 286, 317, 359
410:	296		
411:	40, 110, *147, 162,* 373	433:	350
412:	*147*	434:	241, 350
413:	*73, 109, 147, 258, 358*	435:	*85, 162, 237,* 241, *369 bis*
414:	*109, 228,* 285, 315, *358*	436:	57, *85,* 110, 156, *162,* 314, 325, 332, 350
415:	- -		
416:	*109,* 110, *162,* 188, 342, 350, *358*	437:	*109,* 311, 315, *358,* 373
		438:	311, 315, 350, 359, 373
417:	260, 350	439:	*31 tris,* 57, *85, 109,* 110, 156, *196, 258, 294,* 297, *358*
418:	*162,* 260, 342		
419:	*109, 162,* 181, *358*	440:	57
420:	*162,* 311	441:	*31 tris,* 57, *85, 109,* 110, 156, *237, 244,* 297, 342, 350, *358, 369, 369 bis*
421:	*109,* 110, 181, 282, 331, 342, 350, *358,* 359		
		1424:	350
422:	295, 350	1528:	- -

SUBJECT INDEX

The following index has been prepared in order to help the reader recall where an author, a work, or a theme has been treated in the annotations of this bibliography. It is not, of course, an index of all authors, works, and themes dealt with in the items themselves.

Adgar (writer of French verse miracles): 124

Alfonsine poetry:
Bibliography, contained in other works: 88, 11, 124, 162, 196, 218, 266, 310, 324, 326, 367; issued separately, as a bibliography: 152, 281
Glossaries and word lists: 49, 73, 105, 222, 275, 307
Historical content and value of: 2, 3, 50, 56, 91, 182, 241, 270, 278, 284, 291, 297, 303, 360
Lexical notes on: 57, 76, 80, 232 (arabisms), 241, 247, 293, 300, 311, 325, 328, 332, 336, 369
Translations of:
CSM: 129 (Catalan); 32, 51, 315, 373 (English); 217 (French); 21 (German); 103 (Italian); 4, 92 (Latin); 230 (Portuguese); 3, 49, 50, 62, 63, 153, 304, 372 (Spanish)
Cantigas profanas: 315, 321, 373 (English); 314 (Spanish)
Attributed poems: the Provençal Declaratio (see also Riquier, G.), 309, 327 (Italian); the verse Tesoro, 51 (English)

Alfonso VIII: 44

Alfonso IX: 39, 44

Alfonso X,
Biography of: 137, 162, 189, 196, 211, 217, 237, 297
Devotion to the Virgin: 10, 16, 25 bis, 49, 75, 159, 188
Editor: 71 bis, 90, 231, 355 (see also Cantigas de Santa Maria, under Authorship, and Cantigas profanas, under Authorship)
Legends about: 89, 109, 179, 196
Musicianship of: 1, 28, 79, 169, 186, 217, 238
Poetic court of: 28, 49, 59, 113, 218, 219, 226, 229, 233, 263, 266, 309, 327, 337, 350
Prose works, referred to: General estoria, 90, 111; Primera crónica general, 111; Siete partidas, 19, 111, 180, 330, 344

Folklore in: 246, 268 bis, 272, 313
Formulaic expressions for sources in: 87, 355
Hiatus in: 151, 249
Illumination of: actual plates or drawings, 7, 38, 40 bis, 49, 81, 97, 98, 108,
  113, 140, 174, 176, 200, 220, 243, 256, 263, 279, 288, 289, 335, 353,
  362 bis, 366, 375 bis; artists mentioned, 261, 284, 292; commentary on,
  35, 52, 66, 94, 97, 98, 136, 140, 142, 165, 174, 200, 220, 223, 227, 256,
  266, 269, 279, 289, 292, 302, 315, 330, 335, 353, 362 bis, 365, 366, 375
  bis, 376
Index of names and places of: 132
Inspiration for (from an Arabic collection): 265
Jews in: 319, 338, 345, 347
Language of: Castilian, 9, 13, 25; Galician-Portuguese, 25 bis, 32, 49, 59,
  107, 208, 229, 257, 260, 267, 306; general description of the language
  situation of the Peninsula, 33, 49, 54, 73, 122
Loores of, as a grouping apart from the *miragres:* 12, 25 bis, 51, 62, 95, 107,
  224, 266, 268, 283, 324, 354, 362; basic unity of, 354; *festas de Santa
  Maria* should be considered *loores*, 283
Manuscripts of: descriptions, 22, 49, 149; eye-witness accounts of, 2, 3, 7, 8,
  9, 14, 53; history of, 17, 289; lost MSS of, 88; manuscript of Florence,
  46, 97, 98, 103, 255, 292; manuscript of Toledo, now at Madrid, 108 (a
  facsimile).
Metrics and versification of: 5, 6, 10, 14, 18, 23, 28, 49, 55, 59, 61, 65, 67,
  82, 83, 84, 155, 177, 194, 221, 224, 251, 266, 315, 337; special problems
  of when combined with a study of the music, 79, 224, 299, 340
Music of: studies and comments, 25, 31 bis, 43, 63, 72, 79, 106, 108, 112,
  115, 128, 129, 130, 133, 138, 143, 144, 145, 160, 168, 169, 171, 173,
  176, 181, 184, 185, 186, 191, 193, 198, 199, 205, 206, 213, 215, 236,
  238, 239, 243, 250, 257, 266, 267, 271, 271 bis, 288 (facsimiles), 290,
  315, 321, 354, 366; transcriptions of, 25, 31, 63, 71, 72, 96, 102, 108,
  116, 128, 129, 146, 170, 183, 212, 312, 316
Muslims in: 319, 338, 339, 356
Nasaï resonance in: 334
Personal elements in: 87, 88, 90, 107, 233, 253, 265, 315, 324, 354
Prose versions of (in margin of Escurial MS T.j.l): 280, 364, 371, 372, 375
Provençal presence in: 23, 24 bis, 59, 88, 110, 224
Scholarship of, assessed: 49, 54, 69, 87, 185 (the music), 233, 299
Sources and analogues: 34, 41, 42, 43, 47, 48, 49, 68, 74, 100, 101, 117,
  119, 121, 123, 124, 125, 131, 135, 154, 157, 164, 187, 190, 191, 204,
  207, 225, 234, 235, 240, 254, 257, 263, 274, 346, 367
Strophic forms (combined with music at times): *ballade*, 181; *conductus*,
  206; *rondeau*, 144, 166, 181, 305; *seguidilla*, 194, 221; *virelai*, 144, 173,
  181, 221, 248, 288, 305; *zéjel* form, 206, 214, 305, 340, 348

INDEX OF SCHOLARS